ENGAGING THE SACRED

Smyth & Helwys Publishing, Inc.
6316 Peake Road
Macon, Georgia 31210-3960
1-800-747-3016
©2018 by Kate Anderson
All rights reserved.

Author's Note:
To protect the privacy of all involved, I have changed both
the name of the residential facility where I ministered
and the names of the people who live there.

Library of Congress Cataloging-in-Publication Data

Names: Anderson, Kate A., author.
Title: Engaging the sacred : relational spirituality as pastoral care / by
Kate Anderson.
Description: Macon : Smyth & Helwys, 2019. | Includes bibliographical
references.
Identifiers: LCCN 2018026533 | ISBN 9781641730624 (pbk. : alk. paper)
Subjects: LCSH: Pastoral care. | Interpersonal relations--Religious
aspects--Christianity. | Church work with people with mental disabilities.
| Church work with people with disabilities.
Classification: LCC BV4335 .A53 2018 | DDC 259/.42--dc23
LC record available at https://lccn.loc.gov/2018026533

Advance Praise for *Engaging the Sacred*

The fact that Kate Anderson found Relational Spirituality as the best theological and conceptual system to describe and guide her pastoral work with adults with intellectual and developmental disabilities is not surprising. It may be new to others, but it is a great match in a world where relationships trump conceptual ability all of the time. What is surprising is that she and others then faithfully followed the implications of that spirituality to build a framework for all of the caregiving at the faith-based facility where she was one of the chaplains, discovering along the way that it both matched and encouraged the emotional attachments and sense of reciprocity between staff at all levels and the people they supported, and for staff, between each other. If you want to know what difference faith-based care can provide, here it is.

—Bill Gaventa
Director, Summer Institute on Theology and Disability

The Reverend Kate Anderson shares with us insights she has gleaned from her ministry among those segregated as "intellectually disabled," as well as from her own life, struggles, and faith. Whether you are in a formal pastoral care setting or simply a child of God in the pews and in the world, *Engaging the Sacred* will have you believing in the miraculous, Divine power found in our relationships and lived experiences. May we all learn to "invest in the spirit" of one another.

—Bert Montgomery
Pastor, University Baptist Church, Starkville, Mississippi
Author of *A Rabbi & a Preacher Go to a Pride Parade* and
Of Mice and Ministers

Engaging the Sacred provides a fresh perspective on the transformational power of unconditional positive regard and of seeing the Christ image in others while operationalizing I-Thou relationships with an often underserved population. Kate Anderson's stories of struggles with institutional systems, cultural bias, and theological blind spots provide us with a fresh approach to spiritual care with all persons, especially those who are developmentally delayed. The interdisciplinary application of relational spirituality offers hope in the midst of our health care crises and its overworked staff and financially strapped budgets. Her scriptural foundations and theological reflections make this a must-read for spiritual caregivers in hospitals, care homes, and local parish settings.

—G. Wade Rowatt
ACPE Certified Clinical Educator
Senior Professor, Pastoral Care and Counseling
Baptist Seminary of Kentucky, Georgetown, Kentucky

RELATIONAL SPIRITUALITY AS PASTORAL CARE

ENGAGING
THE
SACRED

KATE ANDERSON

Dedicated to
Chip, Georgia, and Shelby Anderson.
Thank you for giving me the time to offer my truth.
I am so grateful that God saw fit to make you my family.

Acknowledgments

Special gratitude to the individuals who have shaped and supported me along my journey in life and ministry. Thank you for caring when you didn't have to.

Virginia Young Lay
Debra Baker Harman
Daniel & Paige Weeks
Phil & Melanie Rector
Christy Emerson
Mike & Billie Trammel
Brian & Holly Miller
Tommy Valentine
Wade & Jodi Rowatt
Marvin & Julia Tate
Mark Whitsett
Chris Stevenson
Cassandra Tembo
Greg & Jackie Barr
Glenn Williams
Nina Maples
Leslie Townsend
Sister Margaret Ann Hagan
Denise Massey
Loyd Allen
Rob Nash
Sina Rogers
Toni Crouch
Bruce & Mitzi Quick

CONTENTS

Part 1

Relational Spirituality as a Clinical Framework for Pastoral Care

FROM HERE TO THERE: HOW THIS JOURNEY BEGAN

Throughout my research of spirituality as a central element of the human creature, I have found the opportunity to engage many audiences in dialogue. The concept of "person-centered care" within the industry of intellectual disability service providers is more than an interest; it is now a federal standard of care. In the conferences and trainings I provide to colleagues in the field of pastoral care at local, regional, and national conventions, I refer to the human spirit as the ultimate difference between simply meeting standardized "spiritual care" goals and supporting a human being.

While offering training as a guest clinician for a residential facility for people with intellectual and developmental disabilities, I came face to face with the reason I feel compelled to teach spiritual support—support that honors the Divine Investment within all human beings—as an essential element of the care provided for those with intellectual disabilities.

My colleague and I were in the midst of touring this agency. We wanted to gain some sense of context before offering our training session with staff, and this tour was wholly eye-opening. We entered one of the homes on their campus; it was clean and aesthetically pleasing, with bright lighting and current décor. Despite the home's pleasant appearance, the two young staff members responsible for caring for more than twelve residents sat talking and laughing with each other in a room away from the residents. In the program room, one of the men took my hand and repeatedly asked me to help him because urine had saturated his brief, soaking his pants and seeping into his chair cushion. Another resident, sitting in a corner, had taken her shirt off and was playing with the buttons while mouthing the sleeve. I was appalled and heartbroken. The staff, who didn't seem overtly malicious or uncaring, were young, underpaid, and overwhelmed. I could be angry with them only to a degree; these were institutional problems, and the staff hadn't been given the tools they needed to be successful.

When we moved out of the program room, I spotted a young woman (I'll call her Rebecca) at the end of a hallway. Small in stature, she wore pink sweatpants, a lavender sweatshirt, and a pink football helmet. She was repeatedly banging her head against the wall by a window, leaning on the window frame for support. This behavior sometimes occurs in those with autism or intellectual and developmental disabilities (IDD) and can be a result of pain, frustration, or over- or under-stimulation. I asked the staff why she was banging her head. The only answer was, "That's normal for her. It's why she has that helmet. She's fine." My heart sank; not only was such behavior normal for this young lady but the institution's response was a *football helmet* instead of the correct therapeutic headwear to protect her against such self-injurious behavior. I walked over to her and placed my flat hand between her head and the wall as a cushion, just as I have done hundreds of times for my daughters as they crawled too close to a table's edge. She pressed her head into my hand and held it there for a moment. Then she looked up at me with bright, glass-blue eyes. It took a few seconds for her to focus on my face and process my presence with her. When I could see that she was with me, I smiled and said, "Hello."

She smiled back and then leaned away from the window and into my arms, steadying herself on me, taking hold of my arm for stability as she walked. She then accompanied us on the rest of our tour. I thanked her for letting us see her beautiful home. Then I received a free and fully enveloping hug with that pink football helmet laid upon my chest. She offered a "thank you" in American Sign Language.

After our group finished the tour, I retreated to the nearest restroom in the community center next door. I entered quickly, locked the door behind me, and bowed my head in a sorrowful, wordless prayer. My heart was broken when I contemplated my ignorance of the world some people have to endure. I had been devastated by the man whose pants were wet and by the semi-clothed woman chewing her shirt. I had been humbled by Rebecca's response to my simple smile and hello. I felt as if I had invited her into a peaceful, engaging circumstance, and I let her know she was not invisible.

Every person needs to be seen and known; that need is part of our human condition. Goals and objectives can be accomplished without acknowledging the whole person, but an investment in the spirit is required if we are to nurture human beings toward their best selves. The world moves so quickly that we seldom intentionally engage another soul. That engagement begins with seeing each person in their need, their beauty, their wholeness.

The experience of this tour defined my purpose and became the starting place of an assessment tool that works to emphasize the individuality of each soul. With this new clarity, I lifted a prayer of supplication. I pleaded to the God who can accomplish more than I can fathom: "God, help me be part of a world that sees each person's need and does not rely on pink football helmets. Help me teach others to see beyond what we expect to see. Help me understand how we can overlook a whole person. I know we can do better by you. Help me help others like you helped me. Help me help us all. Amen."

That prayer is where the journey of my doctoral work and this book began. I pray that the faith I have found, expressed in a clinical language surrounding that faith, offers something helpful in the path toward helping us all.

Called to the Work of the Soul

On September 16, 2011, I became part of the pastoral services department at Hickory Ridge, an intermediate care facility in Louisville, Kentucky. Offering spiritual support to the people with intellectual disabilities living at Hickory Ridge is my vocational focus. My calling is to provide this support in a way that honors God's investment in the lives of all people. I refer to this concept of *imago Dei*, literally "image of God," as "Divine Investment."

Hickory Ridge is an organization founded in 1970 to support people with intellectual disabilities. The individuals receive various levels of assistance ranging from twenty-four-hour clinical and medical support in intermediate care facilities to evening support in homes we own to weekly visits from job coaches. We provide support for more than 300 people throughout Louisville, Kentucky, and surrounding counties (of those, only about 110 live at Hickory Ridge). We employ nearly 1,000 people and operate with an annual budget of approximately 11 million dollars. A

Christian-based organization rooted in the Missouri Synod Lutheran tradition, Hickory Ridge serves individuals of all faiths and cultures. Three hundred and fifty thousand dollars of the annual budget is allocated to pastoral and spiritual life support. There are now three people in our pastoral services department who provide services across the entirety of Hickory Ridge in various capacities.

My primary focus is assessment, training, and spiritual life program design within the setting of our intermediate care facilities. Hickory Ridge was the first functional property for our organization. It is classified as an intermediate care setting. The facility offers on-campus educational programming, medical care, and clinical therapies. Hickory Ridge is home to seventy-one adults with intellectual disabilities who also have significant health complications. The individuals we support at Hickory Ridge in particular have standardized classifications of "severe" or "profound" cognitive impairment. While many factors contribute to differential assignment of these classifications, the most familiar understanding for people to reference is the IQ. The majority of the people living at Hickory Ridge have a measurable IQ between 30 and 40; a score between 90 and 115 is considered average. I should mention that some individuals served at Hickory Ridge have IQs that are not measurable. This is usually assumed to be a score of less than 20. Many assume that this type of intellectual impediment would limit all comprehension of abstract concepts of faith and spirituality; they are mistaken.

Early in my tenure, I was asked to provide pastoral assessments for these individuals. The standardized assessments I found in pastoral care literature did not adequately accommodate the special needs of the people I had come to know and cherish. I did use some templates and standardized assessments for reference, but none contained the details or information I learned from interviewing and observing the seasoned direct support professionals (DSPs) who had upheld the work of Hickory Ridge for decades. My supervisor, Rev. Dr. Mark Whitsett, provided resources for research, time, and space to synthesize what I found, and he also guided me in my work. My pastoral care training led me to look deeper than standard assessments.

I was looking to identify the details my intuition allowed me to see. With the help of Dr. Whitsett and in relationship with those working and living at Hickory Ridge, I formed an assessment that focused on communicating personhood. The template for that assessment is included in the appendix and is followed by a sample assessment for reference. The root of this assessment was found in an approach to pastoral care support that

Steven Sandage and F. LeRon Shults identified as Relational Spirituality (in *Transforming Spirituality: Integrating Theology and Psychology*, published in 2006). Shults is professor of theology and philosophy at the University of Agder in Norway. Dr. Steven Sandage is a licensed psychologist and professor of psychology and religion at Boston University. Relational Spirituality suggests that "a person's spirituality is the form of his or her life, whether anemic or energetic, anxious or peaceful, in relation to self, other, and God."[1] Where I serve, the fewer words that are attached to something tangible, the better the communication. This definition leads to an understanding of God that does not mandate believers to work so diligently on articulating everything in theological vernacular. At Hickory Ridge, the theological banter I gained at seminary gets in the way of transcendent truth. The growth of the spirit here is found in authenticity, acceptance, and vulnerable attachment to those I am called to support. The culture of my clients has required me to find another way to approach speaking and teaching matters of the human soul. The closest ideology I found to fit the culture of Hickory Ridge was that of Relational Spirituality.

The tangible manifestations of a spiritual support program founded in Relational Spirituality may seem negligible to outside observers. However, the subtle nuance creates a lasting difference in the relationships of our residents and staff. The education and training aspects create an environment full of nuanced grace. In working with staff and the people we support, we emphasize the Divine Investment that is within every life. I define Divine Investment as the energy put forth by the Creator in the existence of each creature. It is a concept that I closely align with Socratic theology, but without the implications of dualism or definitive identification of a portion of identity that is separate from the human soul. When communicating the concept to the people we support, I offer this definition of spirit/soul:

> Our sparkly part is that part of somebody you meet that shows you the bright spots in their eyes or that tickling in your gut when you hug somebody you love. That is the magical part of us that God made. It does not die. Seizures or diseases or differences can't hurt it; our sparkly part is how God shines through us and teaches the world about the good stuff we have to give.[2]

The definition is simple because it must be in the context where I work. How our residents live out their soul identity makes a large difference in our programming and systemic function. How our staff understands the definition of spirituality holds just as much weight.

The individuals living at Hickory Ridge have waivers and funding to support our work because they need intensive support to survive and function in the world. Their dependence is something our clinicians approach with great care. We emphasize personal liberties, choices, empowerment, and life outside of our walls. Consequently, the spiritual aspect of our support is interwoven with daily life, continuing education, and relationships. The pastoral services department works in conjunction with members of an interdisciplinary team. We review monthly trips, recruit spiritual life companions for those who have no remaining family, and incorporate each individual's favorite things into their care programs. The recommendations and suggested special services from our extremely detailed assessment provide a tool for our clinical support areas to use in constructing unique, person-centered support for our residents. Our programmatic framework provides freedom of spiritual nurture for individuals who never had the opportunity to develop a personal religious culture. Many of the individuals living at Hickory Ridge have significant sensory defenses and experience tremendous discomfort in a congregational setting. For these individuals, we schedule individualized spiritual nurture with pastoral staff. The specific preferences or needs of an individual instruct us on how to use the structured pastoral time, for instance by walking nature paths, singing hymns in the chapel, or running laps around the facility. The formula for this program is not difficult, but it is difficult to translate into a blanket course of action. This type of support focuses on the personhood and relationships of people, not on objectives and compliance. There is no single formula for anyone, but there are building blocks to construct a formulaic function for each person. Those essential building blocks are our life story, how we communicate and engage the world around us, and the most effective way for each of us to nurture meaningful relationships.

Early in our program reconstruction, I discovered that the stories of people we support help me formulate a deeply held connection and sense of respect for their personhood. I was fortunate to be one of a few staff members who had the opportunity to look deeply at every person's life story. I discovered that sharing the stories I found, and the details jotted down by their parents at the time of admission, also helped my colleagues develop a relationship with our residents. A primary emphasis in implementing this framework is that God created the human soul with an innate inclination toward the souls of others. That is a prominent theme in the Relational Spirituality construct. Consequently, implementing this structure has required training on self-awareness, interpersonal communication development, and definition of obscure concepts within the realm of spirituality.

Recognizing the various methods of communication in every relationship is imperative. A significant number of the people we support at Hickory Ridge are considered nonverbal, which simply means that standard, articulate conversations are not possible. While working with these individuals, I developed a shorthand guide to deciphering nonverbal communications and demonstrations of anxiety, excitement, sadness, etc.

How do any of us receive kindness and interaction? Grace and kindness are essential in the process of getting to know all people. These adaptations are helpful social engagements. Every individual supported by Hickory Ridge has an "interpersonal notation" section with his or her Spiritual Life Assessment. This section of the assessment lets an unfamiliar person know if someone requires extra personal space due to sensory defenses or if there is a specific posture that helps ease anxiety. It explains whether the individuals prefer playful banter or quiet time with those who matter. It emphasizes the personalities and social preferences that are most conducive to success.

Notes

1. Steven Sandage and F. LeRon Shults, *Transforming Spirituality: Integrating Theology and Psychology* (Grand Rapids MI: Baker Academic, 2006) 67.

2. Kate Anderson, "What God Made," sermon given at Hickory Ridge, LaGrange KY, 6 September 2015 (transcript).

Chapter 1

BIBLICAL, HISTORICAL, AND THEOLOGICAL FOUNDATIONS OF RELATIONAL SPIRITUALITY

This chapter will explore historical, biblical, and theological elements of Relational Spirituality as foundations of pastoral care and human relationships. This chapter will address the theological themes surrounding human relationships and pneumatology (the study of the Holy Spirit) with people who have intellectual and developmental disabilities. Relational Spirituality is an approach to understanding spirituality that integrates psychology and theology in the study of the soul. I want not only to put various elements of theology and behavioral sciences in dialogue but also to make certain those elements remain distinct in a caregiver's understanding of a whole person. To understand and apply Relational Spirituality, we need to understand how these elements—biblical, historical, and theological—work together.

Historical Roots of Relational Spirituality

The relationship between the church and individuals with disabilities has long been complicated. Many members of the early church considered deformities, illness, and disabilities to be byproducts of sin, curses from a vengeful God.[1] However, as Christians better understood the medical science behind many of these anomalies, compassion replaced judgment. The tangible compassion of the Incarnate Christ influenced Christian behavior, and people with disabilities were invited into the community of faith.

As the influence of Jesus' teachings spread across the world, the Church had paradoxical responses to people with disabilities. Throughout the Middle Ages and Roman era, some sects of Christianity supported and offered assistance to individuals with disabilities. Other groups believed the disability, or extreme difference, was the result of the individual's (or their parents') sinful behavior. This viewpoint led some communities to shun these individuals, leave them to die, or even murder them outright in order to conquer the evil that was associated with their existence. In the modern era, science replaced superstition as physical, neurological, and medical processes were better understood. Instances of redemptive care were regarded as mimicry of the Incarnate Christ.[2]

In the Creation account depicted in Genesis, loneliness was the first thing that God declared "not good" (Gen 2:18, NRSV). God saw that the human creature needed connection, not just to nature for nourishment and care, not just to an almighty Creator, but also to other human beings. Human beings must realize an essential truth human beings to find the fullness of spiritual wellbeing. We are shaped, upheld, and challenged by the relationships we form. Relational Spirituality integrates theological and psychological elements of human existence into a common theme of identity. The concept finds its origins in the writing of clinician John Heron in 2001. Heron wrote, "A person manifests the creative process of divine becoming as an autonomous being, embedded in connectedness, and in cooperative, transformative relations with other persons similarly engaged."[3] In 2007, LeRon Shults and Steven Sandage elaborated on Heron's perceptions and theory. Sandage and Shults described the concept of Relational Spirituality in terms of integrating perceived identity in relationship to the "self," to other (community, family, etc.), and to God, a higher power, or greater whole:

Our interdisciplinary approach is an explicit attempt to engage the broader turn to relationality that shapes the conceptual space within which most contemporary philosophical and scientific discourse now occurs. . . . We are not simply integrating abstract bodies of knowledge in psychology and theology but creating a personal relationship as a psychologist and theologian. So the integrative process challenges our own relational spirituality as we surrender the ideal of disciplinary omnipotence and move toward the goal of mutual recognition.[4]

Before we implemented the Relational Spirituality framework at Hickory Ridge, the concept had never been implemented in a strategic fashion. However, there have been descriptions of similar approaches, dubbed "relationship building" and "inclusion." Educational specialist Erik Carter in his work at Vanderbilt University described this strategic implementation of relationship nurture in educational settings. Dr. Carter refers to his intentional support structure as "Peer Support Arrangements" and writes,

> Peer support arrangements differ somewhat from other peer-mediated interventions in their focus and logistics. First, they emphasize support of both academic and social engagement. This differs from peer tutoring, which adopts a more instructional focus on academic skill building, and peer buddy programs, which tend to emphasize social and leisure activities. Second, peer support arrangements are individually tailored interventions that involve a small number of peers rather than an entire class. Peer support arrangements can usually be implemented without changing instructional approaches for the whole class.[5]

Carter describes five steps in the implementation of peer support relationships in the educational setting. We adapted the steps to fit the context of Hickory Ridge and the holistic approach of our Spiritual Life Support Program. Carter's structural map is overlaid with the emotional connections described in Relational Spirituality theory. The relationships formed are part of the work and well-being of the DSPs at Hickory Ridge.

TABLE 1: Comparison of Peer Support Plan and Relational Spirituality Support Program

Peer Support Plan	Relational Spirituality Supports
Step 1: Develop a Peer Support Plan	Step 1: Develop a Spiritual Life Assessment and Support Plan
Step 2: Select and Invite Peer Partners	Step 2: Form Collaborative Relationships across Disciplines to Foster Global Effectiveness
Step 3: Orient Students to Their Roles	Step 3: Orient DSPs to Their Roles as Support and Advocate
Step 4: Work Together during Class	Step 4: Intentional Engagement with DSPs to Gain Input/Feedback for Programming
Step 5: Facilitate Interactions and Support	Step 5: Continuous Facilitation of Support and Interactions (Taking into Account Attrition and the Dynamic Nature of the Human Condition)

This work establishes caregivers' professional responsibility (in spiritual care or otherwise) to incorporate intentional emotional attachment. Training in this approach to care incorporates an intentional focus on the narrative of an individual's life journey. Intentionally knowing an individual creates a deep emotional connection and helps caregivers recognize the humanity of each individual. The human connection also creates a neuronal connection that allows for a change in identity, no matter what the capacity of cognition may be for each person. This is how deep change, on a spiritual level, happens, in reciprocity of giving and receiving.

The Theology of the Human Connection

The effects of human connection are intricately woven into our being. The theological ties that form the tapestry of human existence are established in the handiwork of our Creator. Each of us needs active relationships with others to survive this existence. Dan Siegel describes the connections between our awareness within relationships and our brains as the "mind." He has done a great deal of research surrounding the neurobiology of human interaction and awareness. In his book, *Pocket Guide to Interpersonal Neurobiology: An Integrative Handbook of the Mind*, he writes,

> Once we say that the mind is both embodied and relational, it means that to know our minds we need to know about the body, including the nervous system that is distributed throughout, and interacts with, the entire body . . . . The mind is influenced by, indeed fundamentally created in part by, our social interactions as well as our relationships with entities beyond our bodily selves, with experiences we have with the environment surrounding us. In this way we can say that the mind is both embodied and it is embedded in our relational worlds.[6]

Part of the human design includes the need for human relationship. Relationship and caring are cornerstones of the human experience within the body of Christian Scripture. Human connection is necessary to survive. We are made to need one another. In the twelfth chapter of Paul's letter to the Romans, there is a framing of this interconnectedness.

> For by the grace given to me I say to everyone among you not to think of himself more highly than he ought to think, but to think with sober judgment, each according to the measure of faith that God has assigned. For as in one body we have many members, and the members do not all have the same function, so we, though many, are one body in Christ, and individually members one of another. Having gifts that differ according to the grace given to us, let us use them: if prophecy, in proportion to our faith; if service, in our serving; the one who teaches, in teaching; the one who exhorts, in his exhortation; the one who contributes, in generosity; the one who leads, with zeal; the one who does acts of mercy, with cheerfulness. (Rom 12:3-8, CEV)

The authors of Christian history note that isolation is so cataclysmic to human beings that Godself deemed it the first imperfection in need of repair (Gen 2:6-7, 18). Throughout the Judeo-Christian story, there have been several theologians who offered perspectives on the interconnectedness of human beings. Theologian Thomas E. Reynolds offers commentary regarding human beings in relationships as part of a Divine process of co-creation:

Humankind is fundamentally relational. We are caught up in a web of interdependence with the created world, inescapably dependent upon creation for sustenance and well-being. As the creative power of God extends itself in relationship with others, so does the *Imago Dei*. Creative power essentially is a relational power.

Fundamental to human relationality is a material, bodily existence. We do not have bodies; we are our bodies. Human beings are living souls, not souls trapped in a material body, but organically unified, embodied creatures. And our bodies define our limits. To deny this is to deny our relationship to other creatures, for relationships depend upon the differentiation created by bodily limits. Furthermore, denying the body denies the God who lovingly sculpted it from the earth. . . . Our bodies are woven into the fabric of creation, connecting us to the elements in a way that makes us a part of the dynamic interdependence of all things.[7]

Reynolds points to a critical interdependence between all people, extending to all of creation and offers implications of the interdependence on our emotional, spiritual, and physical well-being. This interdependence is accentuated in the lives of individuals with disabilities because of their physical and social dependence while trying to function in daily life. Reynolds also challenges many presumptions regarding ontological (the study of why humanity exists) value and productivity that are related to Western culture. The motivation and rewards relative to doing "good works" in Christian culture have affected how we assess human value. In this framework, people living with significant disabilities are considered to be lesser human beings because of their lack of tangible productivity. Reynolds challenges this concept by suggesting a different metric of value altogether—one of equitable, intrinsic value for every person made by God.

Jesus's ministry embodies divine love through what we have been calling a metaphorical reversal. The center is not the strong but the weak, not those who have it all but those who are without, not the privileged but the disinherited, not the insider but the outsider. . . . Jesus's ministry upsets the order. Through Jesus the creator God comes to us not as what we might expect—a possessing, domineering, displacing, or controlling presence—but rather in the form of self-giving love, inviting or luring us into relational creativity and wholeness. . . . It is not scarcity that governs the kingdom of God but abundance. God's love knows none of the conventional distinctions between "pure" and "impure" or "good" and "bad." The kingdom of God is radically inclusive.[8]

Reynolds challenges the cultural perspective that elevates social perception, or position, based on a hierarchical structure related to productivity. This unique perception is found in Jesus' blessing of the children, the infirm, and the disenfranchised throughout the Gospels. Simply said, God does not have favorites. No life contributes more or less to the world because of differences in productivity. Each soul is precious; all people, regardless of material productivity, reveal elements of the sacred through the living of their lives. Behavioral sciences and theology offer us lenses through which we can better understand more pieces of an incomprehensible whole: God's radically inclusive love and value of every soul.

Theology of Community in Covenant

Paul was the first, outside of Jesus the Christ, to mandate our need to remain in community. In Romans 12, Paul reframes the church's understanding of community. Here he brings a tone of Grecian philosophy and Judaic theology into the scaffolding of his ecclesiology. According to the *Mercer Commentary on the Bible*, the new perspective on "love" and connection is rooted in a transformative, sacrificial comprehension of what it means to be a Christian. Richard F. Wilson writes,

> That love should be genuine takes on here a thematic significance. Heretofore in Romans Paul has used the term *agape* of God's love in its surprising concern for the radically underserving. Now Paul uses agape for the love that believers should extend both to fellow members of the body and to enemies of the outside. The love that believers have received they are to share.
>
> For Paul love as an ethical disposition and mode of action means to see the good or advantage of the other person rather than one's own. Paul expresses this in a number of places and with different vocabulary. This central ethical norm is an open or formal one. What constitutes the good of the other is left undefined and is to be determined in differing social contexts. In this particular passage seeking the advantage of the other takes such expressions as showing honor, meeting physical needs, emotional identification, living in harmony, and renouncing vengeance. Love does not passively accept evil but overcomes it.[9]

Romans 12 is one of the epistle passages that help human beings gain a greater understanding of their identity when they enter into covenant with other members of the faith as well as the Body of Christ, the church. In this chapter of Scripture, selfless love requires mutuality to be genuine. Prior to this point in history, the concept of sacrificial love was not widely addressed outside of the gospel and the prophetic moments of Old Testament Scripture pointing toward the Incarnation. The Pauline identification of love's reciprocal responsibility between members of the human race helped establish a new platform for caring in community.

This interconnectedness is highlighted in relationships with individuals with IDD. There is a clear vulnerability present when engaging in relationships with individuals who have severe intellectual and physical disabilities. They need help to survive, but they do not apologize for their open need. Neither do most people with IDD consider their need for support a major flaw in their identity, at least not often. There are no apologies for the need for support because there is an awareness that every person needs other people. Whether it is opening a door, putting away dishes, offering a hug, or saying a prayer with someone, acts of kindness offered to and by individuals (both with and without disabilities) are signs of the relational equality they have experienced. Relational equality is subtle and important to recognize, and it is easily missed if the recipient does not slow down to recognize the gift. At the core of Hickory Ridge Lodge, when we recognize the spectacular Divine Investment in each person, we see with eyes open to each person's God-given beauty. Again, Divine Investment is defined as the investment of the Creator's energy and imagination in the formation of each living creature. Recognizing and engaging this semblance of *imago Dei* in its fullness, we are invited to respond with a tapestry of multifaceted grace that develops our own faith-building process.

Theology in a Different Language

The concept of Relational Spirituality is even more suitable for the context of Hickory Ridge because of some residents' limited cognitive processes. These cognitive differences have no bearing on the value of the soul. The cognitive struggles of those in my congregation simply point to the necessity for a different understanding or manner of communication. Theological concepts and abstract ideology may not lend themselves well to individuals with significant intellectual disabilities, but the process of building faith and relationships is a means of communicating what the spoken word cannot communicate. At Hickory Ridge, the language of God's identity, investment, and care is communicated through actions of supportive, nurturing relationship. Our program design is fine-tuned to the individual need of each soul we support.

Temple Grandin writes about her experience of information synthesis as an autistic person in *Thinking in Pictures: My Life with Autism*:

> I am a person who learns by concrete examples. . . . There were two things we did at church that had meaning to me. Every Christmas, each child had to take one of his or her really nice toys and wrap it up as a Christmas gift for a poor child. At the service the minister stood in front of a manger filled with presents and said, "It is better to give than to receive." This made a big impression . . . . Abstract religious concepts will not be understood by many individuals on the spectrum. It is better to teach them how to be good citizens through a series of hands-on activities.[10]

Grandin makes the concepts of spirituality relative to human experience and shows us how to apply them in practical ways. She points out the need to create tangible evidence for individuals who struggle with abstract concepts. In the Relational Spirituality construct, those tangibles are connected with more than just understanding; they are also reinforced with emotional experience. This reality makes their impact even more profound for all participants.

God Made Known in Harmony

The Relational Spirituality framework intentionally integrates this theology and psychology in every employee's training. Hickory Ridge was born out the need of six families who had children with severe intellectual disabilities. These families scrimped, saved, and advocated their way to create a safe, healthy environment for their children, which was not what they found when they sought out placement in state facilities at that time. This group established Hickory Ridge in 1970. The families worked diligently to raise funds, create awareness, and form collaborative partnerships that became the foundation of our organization.

Much of the culture of Hickory Ridge is a direct result of the failures of other institutional settings in the late twentieth century. The quality of medical interventions improved so that more complicated medical processes were no longer seen as terminal diagnoses. Conditions such as Down syndrome, autism, and cerebral palsy were still significant, but the infants, adolescents, and adults with significant disabilities were surviving at a higher rate. The funding provided for institutional settings was not sufficient to provide adequate resources for growing populations of the institutions in the United States.[11]

It is not uncommon to find employees of Hickory Ridge who have been on staff since it opened its doors. Many of our direct support staff can tell the stories of the people we support because they were welcomed into the families who built the organization. There are many who have become guardians of the people we support after their retirement and the deaths of all other family members. Our organization is unique because the support staff has nurtured intimate, emotional connections with the residents. Their ability to recognize and receive the gifts offered by the people we support is the sacred element that separates this organization from many others of its kind. It is easy to witness the connection and relate that loving kindness to God, but it is a difficult concept to articulate in theological terms. LeRon Shults describes the theological quandary:

> The "personality" of God in the New Testament is not depicted in terms of the autonomous self-sufficiency of a divine individual but in terms of the loving relations among the Father, Son, and Holy Spirit. Finally, the Spirit of the Biblical God is not described in mechanical terms as a first efficient cause but as a promising presence that calls creatures into being and toward fellowship in the arriving reign of divine peace. The best way to conserve the intuitions of the Biblical tradition about the concept of "spirit" is to liberate them for transforming dialogue in our cultural location. As we participate in this ongoing task, we remain committed to upholding the distinction between finite creaturely spirit and infinite Creator Spirit, to integrating the Trinitarian relations within our understanding of the Spirit, and to accounting for the eschatological dimension of redemptive experience—being called toward a share in the eternal life of God.[12]

In Schultz's depiction of our task to process relationships in a theological framework, he incorporates a parallel process of joining in a relational kinship with the Trinitarian God. There is me and there is you, and in our midst is a holy connection that is God. Even differing faith traditions find a kinship in this perception of a higher power or a greater whole. In this way, a Relational Spirituality framework provides a common language between different systems of belief and cultures.

This concept of spirituality is similar to harmonic structures in music. There is one note and there is another note; each has its own identifiable note name and pitch frequency. They are singular and whole as they are, but when they are joined, the connection forms a third element: the harmony. The frequency of each note is still present; the recurrent sound waves maintain their identity. When they are played simultaneously, a miraculous connection takes place as each set of sound waves dance in concert with one another. The sound may be crystal clear and uplifting in timbre, or it may be tight and dissonant to the ear, but the notes that were just one identity and another identity become a third identity when played together. This is how the connection of relationship functions at its basic level. Human beings experience God and life as their own; they are *experts* on their understanding and experience. Then we are drawn toward a connection with others who have their understanding and experience. When we meet with the expertise of one another in healthful community, God creates a consonant third thing that fuels the identity and faith building of each. Sandage and Schultz identify the effects of interpersonal connection in the process of faith formation. There is a dance of awareness that can be described only as sacred when the effects of relationship are considered to be in parallel process with self-identification and our understanding of identity in relationship to a higher power. The authors offer a description of the dance of intimacy:

> Personal attachments emerge within an interpersonal field of mutual binding and being-bound in relation. In this general sense, the human spirit is formed in the context of "faith"—in the pensive struggle to bind oneself to trustworthy relations. This is what Erik Erikson referred to as the "basic trust" that is a condition for the emergence of healthy identity throughout life, and the longing for intimacy that drives human knowing is transformed precisely in and through these relations. Christian faith is an experience of the gracious transformation of this natural longing for truth, an intensification of the desire for intimacy in relation to the Spirit of wisdom, who holds all things together and invites us into the mutual knowing of the Son and the Father. The dynamic process of becoming wise is transforming spirituality. The Colossians are "filled with the knowledge of God's will in all spiritual wisdom and understanding" as they "grow in the knowledge of God" (Colossians 1:9-10). Having been clothed with a new self, "which is being renewed in knowledge according to the image of its creator" (Colossians 3:10), they are urged to live together, teaching and admonishing one another "in all wisdom" as the word of Christ "dwells" in them richly (Colossians 3:16).[13]

The dance creates a drive toward knowing and being known, a part of the human condition. If addressed in terms of faith communities and relationships that mold our understanding of our own identity, the component of reciprocal revelation through dialogue and shared faith experiences is clearly seen. Members of the Christian faith comprehend the identity of God relative to experience. We know the God that lives in our experience. In like kind, we are able to gain a greater insight into the identity of the Almighty when we receive the depiction from another's experience. In this moment, our presence, our relationships, and creative empathy help us gain a multidimensional understanding of God's identity. The clearest demonstration of this theological concept is revealed in the Incarnate Christ, who offered an invitation to see God's character made flesh.

This is an element of pneumatology that addresses the aspects of God present within every life, including the lives of individuals who live with significant disabilities. In my experience, their experiences of God or a higher power may differ from the experiences of people who are neurotypical, and their depiction of God, though the language may differ, is no less beautiful. Experiences of God, as described by a person with IDD, may lack many of the assumptions made by people who do not share their unique perspective.

Defining God, or a higher power, based solely on our own experience and understanding sets up an idolatrous god shaped in our image rather than an awesome, indefinable Deity. Sandage and Schultz write,

> The human spirit longs to understand its relation to the sacred, to interpret the ultimate meaning of its identity in relation to that which is beyond its comprehension. Wisdom has to do with the desire for truth, but this quest is for more than simply a quantitative increase in objective intellectual content or even increased functional competence in the use of knowledge. The longing for wisdom ultimately has to do with the quality of our concrete relations in lived community. If we merely stress the importance of the individual's cognitive assent to propositions, we can easily fall into a limited definition of spiritual maturity that is correlated to how much a person knows "about" God. This can obscure the much more intimate understanding of wisdom in Scripture and the Christian tradition, which emphasized the intimacy of knowing and being known by God in the Spirit.[14]

In my congregation, God does not have to make sense to remain God; my congregants do not have to define God's identity to maintain their faith or their love. I gain invaluable understanding of God by experiencing a life of faith alongside the members of my congregation. One man said to me, "Pastor Kate, I love you for no reason at all. I love you just 'cause you *is*." This is the love of God that humanity needs desperately.

At Hickory Ridge, I am not loved for my degrees or appearance or because I am neuro-typical.

I am loved because I *am*, which my congregation is able to articulate clearly to me. They do not shy away from telling their pastor that she is enough and that God loves her, too. Whether I hold multiple academic degrees or theological certifications—or none—is irrelevant. I am the sister of my congregants, the friend, the pastor, the helper, and the servant. In the relationships formed at Hickory Ridge, there very little regard for personal hierarchy, assumed or stated. The revelation of God's equitable investment in every life has been clarified over and over throughout my five years of service at Hickory Ridge.

Once, religious leaders would have assumed God cursed my congregants with maladies that would permanently separate them from knowing the true nature of the Divine. Their impassioned faith and love for God do not convey this as truth. I am neuro-typical. I seek to understand everything before committing to trust. Do these qualities mean my faith foundation is stronger than the faith foundations of my congregation? The impassioned faith of those I serve tells me that, in fact, I may have less capacity to release my fear so that I may trust in a God I can never fully comprehend. This is the paradox of my ministry at Hickory Ridge; I offer the wisdom and teaching of God as I am able, but I recognize that God is being simultaneously revealed through the questions and care offered by those who call me their pastor. This truth is also present for the direct support staff who assist the individuals at Hickory Ridge through their daily lives.

God Alive in Giving and Receiving

The traditional hierarchy of superiority of clinician over client or of guardian over the people we support seldom plays a part in day-to-day relationships. In the everyday interactions, the people who assist residents in taking their baths, dressing, and using the restroom offer the residents respect and dignity—sometimes to a greater degree than the clinicians who design program plans. In return, the residents offer the direct support staff more respect than they offer the clinicians. The difference in mutual esteem is rooted in the level of relationship.

There is indescribable beauty found in relationship with the individuals supported at Hickory Ridge. Just like people everywhere, the people who call Hickory Ridge home are a wide range of cantankerous, lively, unbreakable spirits. Like people everywhere, our residents have strength of spirit and a strong sense of identity, but there is not a competition surrounding values of productivity or status. In the midst of these relationships, reciprocal authenticity is the greatest value. Living life in the midst of this culture is truly a sacred experience.

The primary emphasis of the pastoral services department at Hickory Ridge is the innate value of human beings, their identity, and the respect of their personhood. This concept is focused both on the people living at Hickory Ridge and on employees who support them. The implementation of Relational Spirituality does not provide room for one-sided intimate connection. Human beings were not created to exist in relationships without balanced contributions, evidence of the nature of a loving God who made us to be loved and to give love simultaneously. Rabbi Bradley Shavit Artson describes it as a kinship of the human spirit and the nature of God:

> God relates to humanity primarily through love—the inviting power to surpass ourselves and to risk growth and innovation. Indeed, God's vulnerability and dynamism are both a manifestation and a consequence of God's love for us and for the world. Recognizing that all living creatures are in a continuing pattern of engagement and connection, we become who we are by our courage to love and to nurture. And we, like God, remain vulnerable and self-surpassing because of our resilient loves.[15]

Understanding God in terms of relationship and connection provides a foundation that every participant can embrace. The relational aspect helps build a bridge of collaboration between believers and nonbelievers for the implementation of Spiritual Life Supports. Those caregivers who do not necessarily profess a belief in the Judeo-Christian God often agree there is "something bigger" that bonds us and that is near while they support the individuals at Hickory Ridge. There is an energy present in the necessary vulnerability and engagement that requires an intentional "presence" in the work we do.

Pastoral care primers teach that the human mind cannot cling to concepts held in abstraction in moments of crises, but we are drawn toward caring, compassionate, outstretched arms to remind us of our place in the realm of all humanity. The reptilian brain is built for survival; even in desperation it will reach for the grasp of a safe ally. This is true for individuals who do not have the cognitive capacity to grasp abstraction. Consequently, the smiles and support of those who care become a tangible reinforcement of God's care for and with the people of Hickory Ridge. Likewise, it is very difficult to relay the experience of God in tangible language for others to understand. The struggle demonstrates some of the dichotomy present in the faith-building of the individuals who make up my congregation. We are active and involved in the world, for certain, but the culture day-to-day life of Hickory Ridge are different from any other I have experienced.

It is difficult to understand the identity of God with words that surround concrete concepts or analogies, but it is easy to understand the identity of God in silence. Many of the individuals in my congregation have limited verbal abilities, and some are completely nonverbal. These individuals still value time with their pastor, but they seldom seek conversation. With these individuals, a pastoral meeting may consist of a walk through the wooded area behind the lodge or just sitting in the stillness of our chapel holding hands.

My time with those who live in silence has taught me that the words we use in our description of God may be valuable, but they can't relay the fullness of God's identity. Words and academic-speak can help people feel a little less powerless, so God makes concession for our frailty in this need. This concession is unnecessary for people who are comfortable with the situation of powerlessness or who do not readily focus on "power" in relationships at all. To these individuals, the power of presence and vulnerability is a reciprocal invitation to worship that is truly free of humanity's frailty; the relational bond creates the sense of a "fourth dimension" in sacred experiences. The fourth dimension moves beyond time, space, and identity; it encompasses the investment of God present within each creature; it is the dimension of connection. God's most profound work is done when hearts and souls make that connection and love without pretense.

The theological aspect of the ministry done alongside individuals with significant IDD is not bound by questions surrounding theodicy or human suffering. Those are theological questions that surface repeatedly for professionals providing spiritual care, but they are not central to the work done as a minister in my context. My theological questions focus on the trust and freedom of the individuals I support. Why do they trust so easily? How can I lean into the limitless love of God with as much certainty as they do? Is the love of God as pure and innocent as the love I encounter here? How do I tame my envy of their understanding of unconditional love, untainted by competition and insecurity? In all these questions the answer is the same. A simple prayer that I offer every day: "God, help me to be more like the congregation I serve."

The knowledge of God that is gained in the midst of the ministry done at Hickory Ridge is one of reciprocity, one of relationship. I show up, as I am, offering who I am; my brothers and sisters who offer the same presence greet me. Together, in relationship, we understand God's love and the intrinsic value of one another just as we are. That reciprocity is the foundation of the title *Engaging the Sacred*. Ministry in the community of Hickory Ridge cannot be offered "to" the people, and it cannot be offered "for" the people. The only way that God's care can truly be invested in this community is if it is offered "with" the community. This is the sacred breath in the midst of my theology.

The ultimate goal of this book's articulation of a Relational Spirituality framework in the field of pastoral care is to replicate this type of spiritual support in other settings. Offering this perspective may provide a route toward integration for pastoral care providers within other social and emotional support professionals.

Notes

1. "History of Disabilities in Brief," PACER Center, http://familieslead.org/files/1414/1296/0207/history_in_brief.pdf (accessed 23 July 2016).

2. Rodney Stark, *The Rise of Christianity* (San Francisco: Princeton University Press, 1996) 182.

3. Jim Heron, *Spiritual Discovery as Divine Becoming* (London: SAGE Publishing, 2001) 39-45.

4. Steven Sandage and LeRon Shults, *Transforming Spirituality: Integrating Theology and Psychology* (Grand Rapids MI: Baker Academy, 2006) 124.

5. Erik W. Carter, "Promoting Inclusion, Social Connections, and Learning through Peer Support Arrangements," *Teaching Exceptional Children* 48/1 (2015): 9-18.

6. Daniel J. Siegel, *Pocket Guide to Interpersonal Neurobiology: An Integrative Handbook of the Mind* (New York: WW Norton & Co, 2012), Kindle edition, ch. 1, par. 18.

7. Thomas E. Reynolds, *A Vulnerable Communion: A Theology of Disability and Hospitality* (Grand Rapids MI: Brazos Press, 2008) 127.

8. Ibid., 221.

9. Richard F. Wilson, "Love in One Body," in *Mercer Commentary on the Bible*, ed. Watson E. Mills, Edd Rowell, and Richard F. Wilson (Macon GA: Mercer University Press, 1996) 1172.

10. Temple Grandin, *Thinking in Pictures: My Life With Autism* (New York: Doubleday, 2006) 142.

11. PACER Center, Inc., "History of Disability in Brief," *Disabilities Resource*, http://familieslead.org/files/1414/1296/0207/history_in_brief.pdf (accessed 12 May 2014).

12. Sandage and Schultz, *Transforming Spirituality*, 37.

13. Ibid., 172.

14. Ibid., 132.

15. Bradley Shavit Artson, *The God of Becoming and Relationship: The Dynamic Nature of Process Theology* (Woodstock: Jewish Lights Publishing, 2013) 89.

Chapter 2

HICKORY RIDGE'S JOURNEY TO A NEW FRAMEWORK OF SPIRITUALITY

In September 2011 my task as the Spiritual Life Program assistant was to complete assessments for every individual supported by Hickory Ridge. My supervisor, Rev. Dr. Mark Whitsett, provided resources for research, time and space to process what I found, and guidance through spiritual growth for me in the process. My pastoral care training led me to look deeper than the standard assessments I found to fill out for the people we support. I was looking for a model that would reinforce my intuition, that could prescribe the loving, nurturing care our seasoned direct support professionals had provided our residents for decades.

With the help of Dr. Whitsett and in relationship with those working and living at Hickory Ridge, I created an assessment that focused on communicating personhood. The root of this assessment was found in an approach of pastoral care support identified as Relational Spirituality. As part of God's providence, Hickory Ridge experienced a change in leadership during our search process. Mr. Christian Stevenson became the president and CEO of the agency. Chris's approach to faith and leadership focused on unity, cooperation, and intentional collaborations, laying fertile ground for the emphasis on Relational Spirituality to take root.

The greatest difficulty in working toward a functional framework of Relational Spirituality is the multidimensional aspect of the implementation. Relationships must be authentic in order to deliver spiritual nurture as intended within this program, but authentic relationships do not happen in a corporate structure without intentional investment in building collegial relationships. Competition and hierarchy are generally the status quo in corporate environments, but our facility was blessed to be an exception to that rule when we were granted the freedom to attempt something unique in the way we provided care.

In their 2006 publication, *Transforming Spirituality: Integrating Theology and Psychology*, LeRon Shults and Steven Sandage provide the foundation of our program by defining spirituality. They write, "A person's spirituality is the form of his or her life, whether anemic or energetic, anxious or peaceful, in relation to self, other, and God."[1]

The first stage of developing an effective model of Relational Spirituality programming was to identify the complex foundation that needed to be in place for implementation. We needed to be proactive in communicating a system-wide value of humanity and the value of investing in the process of vulnerability that this cultural understanding demands. Luckily, we unknowingly built some of that foundation even before we realized how necessary it was. God was working all around us before we recognized the work God would be doing through us.

Chris and the team of senior administrators worked diligently to even the playing field within the social hierarchy of Hickory Ridge and the organization at large. He assembled teams of managers and administrators for exercises to nurture a culture shift in perspective; he scheduled events that celebrated the contribution and value of every member of Hickory Ridge's staff. Chris initiated a shadowing program that meant our corporate vice-presidents were, literally, working shoulder to shoulder with people in maintenance, dietary, housekeeping, and direct care. These experiences created new dynamics of inclusion on every level of our organization. Cultural shifts have to work in reciprocity; the application to base interpersonal skills needs to be universal or any attempt toward social equity could not stand.

The first phase of intentional structure for the pastoral services department was to sculpt an assessment that would be a meaningful tool for relationship building, not just *for* the people we support but also *with* the people we support. We constructed a Spiritual Life Assessment that represented a holistic approach to personhood and spirituality (see pg. 111).

This assessment was designed for the spiritual support of every individual supported by our organization. Compiling the elements of the assessment was a tedious, demanding process. However, the assessment has become a tool for staff members and clinicians within our entire organization. We combined several therapeutic and spiritual elements in the final document. We included a biography of each individual for their caregivers and learned after our training session that the biographies promoted emotional engagement as well as a reciprocal emotional attachment between residents and staff.

Descriptions of nonverbal communication along with sensory needs are included in the interpersonal skills section. Important relationships, preferred activities and places, means of comfort, and suggested special services make up the next section. These details are useful in various areas of individual support. Frequently, we assist in providing support for some of these special services because they are not within the assigned clinical area of any particular department. The inclusion of these elements is a byproduct of care, not just clinical practicum. The final section of the assessment includes notes regarding religious or faith practice that are consistent with the individual's culture or request.

The formalized implementation of the program required a foundation for tracking spiritual wellness of the individuals we support, a means of tracking program effectiveness, and an operational training structure for every member of the staff at Hickory Ridge. The implementation process has been an effort of intentional enculturation of the whole Hickory Ridge system and has taken place in conjunction with the administrative efforts to create an atmosphere of collegial, cooperation, and healthful communications.

I could not have imagined the impact of this assessment and program shift. I believe that God helped cultivate a "perfect time" for all of Hickory Ridge: if not for a director of pastoral care open to finding a model that best fits our context of function, nothing would have come from our frustration with the standard assessments. If not for the hopeful, faith-based perspectives on culture from our CEO, we could not have implemented the systemic collaboration. In this time, in this organization, our situation made way for a special discovery about the power of relationships. One year after implementing the program and training, staff turnover decreased by 15 percent, and there was a notable, positive change in morale. One year after implementing this collaborative, relationally based, holistic support structure, there was a measurable gain in residents' adaptive function, which is the measurement of how people actively engage the world around them. Across the board, every person supported by Hickory Ridge raised their adaptive function score anywhere from 2 to 48 percent. Collaborative ideologies became a prominent part of the organization as a whole, and staff members became more creative in problem-solving and designing supportive activities for the people supported by Hickory Ridge.

Note

1. Steven Sandage and LeRon Shults, *Transforming Spirituality: Integrating Theology and Psychology* (Grand Rapids MI: Baker Academic, 2006) 217, 261.

Chapter 3

THE SANCTITY OF CONNECTION

Human beings were made to participate in this life together. Our identity, actions, and faith are shaped and molded through our interactions with others; our perceptions are broadened and changed in relationships with others. This is where the magic of Relational Spirituality takes place. Our souls are broken and mended in our connection with the other souls we allow to become part of us. This sacred intermingling is where the theoretical root of Relational Spirituality is found.

Relational Spirituality has roots in Relational Development Theory, which describes a means of maturing faith and identity nurtured in connection with other people who journey alongside us. Kaye Cook and Kathleen Leonard describe the Relational Development Theory as dependent on "embodied experience," the level of development that occurs when faith building happens in the context of relationship building. This theory not only allows for exploration of the theological ideologies of an individual but also permits faith exploration of those concepts within the life context of their peers living in diverse contexts. Cook and Leonard describe the necessary integration that takes place in these settings because the theology growth is inseparably joined to the identity formed in relationships, which creates a social mirror of sorts by which those exploring faith can see a trusted reflection of their own identity. The study described in their article validates the necessity for relationship building and fellowship in the life of God's church, for the good of all her members as well as the body of believers as a whole.

The irony is that this study validates a theological presupposition that is foundational to most Western Judeo-Christian systems of belief. In the work of scientists such as Steven Sandage, Jim Heron, LeRon Shults, and Daniel Siegel, there are several pieces of scientifically validated changes that take place within the human mind during the intentional connections we form as we build relationships with one another. Taken together, the work of these scientists (Cook, Leonard, Sandage, Heron, Shults, and Siegel) validates what I have experienced in my work as a pastoral caregiver for nearly two decades. Their validation helps soothe my doubt so that I can continue the work I have been called to do; in this realization I recognize that I am even shaped by relationships I have with people I have never met. This power is at the center of all care offered to support the human soul. It is how we find one another and ourselves in a chaotic, disordered life.

The Sanctity of Our Relationship with a Triune God

Our understanding of God is broadened in relationship with other people; the identity of an Almighty, Creator God has been offered to humanity in terms of relationship. The Triune God has been segmented, at least in a perceptional way, to help us grasp the magnitude of something we would never understand otherwise. We build ourselves and our relationships on previous experience, previous connections, and on our understanding of how people are supposed to connect as we all journey toward becoming who we were made to become. God chose to be known to us through the lens of formative relationships: the Father, Son, and Holy Spirit, three entities revealed as portions of the same Almighty God. The Father is a figure of authority, the giver of life, our protector, our provider. The Incarnate Son is a sibling to our circumstance in his experience of the human condition, a man who lived the challenges of our limitations and experienced the fragility of loving and being loved. The Holy Spirit is One who is present around and within us all as a force of inexplicable magic, mystery, and holiness; it is the source of the inexplicable energies that flow through human relationships. There is a simplistic, raw honesty in attaching such a huge, incomprehensible God to these compassionate terms of identity. Even in the revelations that make a God who authored all of creation something comprehensible, there is a gentle grace teaching us how to love our God and love one another.

The Father

The formative stages of our development contain some of the most magnificent, intricate details of God's design within the human creature. The scientific testing available to us in this era helps us see how quickly cells mature and tissue develops. We are the first generation that gets to benefit from studies detailing the formation of the microscopic chains of DNA unfolding into tissue and electronic connections swirling in a systematic, chaotic explosion that becomes a person we get to encounter, or the person we get to become. I read scientific articles about such events with a logical, clinical understanding of the processes that take place, and I am amazed at the intricacies that current research is able to unfold. However, when I let myself *feel* in the midst of all that *knowing*, I am overwhelmed. The scientific intricacy, yes, but also the inexplicable and the undefinable aspects of God's creation are incomprehensible gifts to us. I fall to my knees in the humble awareness that all of this creative motion took place in the garden with the creation of the first of our genus, then again as I was formed into a life, and then again within my very being as I bore two precious human beings.

The humility I feel when I consider the creation of the human creature is what calls me to my deep respect of the authority of God, my Father. Please forgive the language of antiquity. I use the term "Father" because it is the term used in the New Testament by the Incarnate Christ. I am aware that the gender designation is not necessary to recognize God's authority, but using the vernacular of my early childhood comforts me. For my purposes, the authority that is at the head of the identity of God offers a symbol of supreme authority. This is the character of the Divine that was sought and feared throughout much of the Old Testament Scriptures of Christianity. The God who made us, the God who gave humanity the commandments and order to follow, is the God we serve and fear. This is the God who created the Israelites with a specific purpose in mind, to worship and serve. But is that really the totality of the authority we know for God? I find it difficult to trust deeply in a figure that shows so little of Godself yet asks so much in terms of our trust. This is where I find myself surrendering to the uncomfortable parts of my faith, believing in what I cannot touch or fully comprehend; that, in fact, is how I define "faith."

The Son

Just as the Triune God helps us comprehend God in terms of relationship, God provided Christ to us in relationship. In relationship with the Incarnate Christ, we find a brother. He was born in the midst of humble beginnings, raised by earthly parents who struggled and strived like many people we have known in our lives. From the time Jesus proclaimed truth in the temple at the age of twelve until he breathed his last on the cross, he was misunderstood and rejected by many. We can empathize with this plight and find ourselves seeking some semblance of commonality with an incarnation who was bound by flesh just as we are in life.

In the life of Jesus we also see a man who lived for something bigger than the life he was given. Outside of the miracles that have become pillars of the Christian faith, Jesus lived to lead and teach others about the difference they make. He loved and taught twelve disciples alongside him as he met people along the roads he traveled. These twelve would become his legacy, at least the tangible portion, until their lives ended. They would teach as he taught. They would live lives of integrity and grace, just as he modeled for them. I tell my students that good leaders are gifted in their craft; they studied hard to do the work they were made to do. Great leaders do all of these things too, but they invest their energy in teaching and empowering others to do the same because they know the gifts they were given were not meant to be theirs alone. We have the potential to create so much more than our limitations of time and energy can achieve; living into this kind of faith is to live like Christ, our brother.

The Holy Spirit

The definition and description of the Holy Spirit is much more complicated than the other parts of the Triune God. The Holy Spirit baffles us all because it lacks clear definition, at least in tangible terms. It is a mysterious portion of the human experience, rooted in the feeling of emotions and intuition. The Spirit is within, around, and among us in all areas of our lives. No matter what terminology is used to describe this part of the human experience, there is a consensus that there is something inexplicable that is part of living. I believe that the sanctity of this part of God is found in every soul and draws soul to soul, no matter what the circumstance. We were not made to be separate from one another, but our nature drives the competition and self-preservation that camouflage that truth much of the time.

Trinity of Self-formation

Similar to the elements of a Triune God, I believe that our understanding of ourselves can be conveyed in three parts: relationship to self, relationship to others, and relationship to God, a higher power, or a greater whole. I've associated each aspect of self-identity with a foundational element: freedom, joy, and peace. Balancing these parts of ourselves and these elements is key to our spiritual well-being.

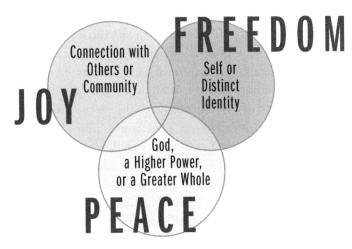

Our categorical "self" construction is based on how we are woven into our world. This representation clearly comes from my Christian world-view, but there is room for an application to individuals who do not claim Judeo-Christian faith. In the assessment I have done with the individuals under my care for spiritual support, I take stock of how their experience of the world may be slanted to throw the diagram off balance. If the triquetra at the center of the diagram is not equally laid, I do my best to prescribe activities or engagement that will help to shift the circles back toward center.

FREEDOM
Knowing who you are and what you value,
and advocating for the life you choose for yourself.

Connection to our "self" cultivates a freedom to live out our true identity without fear of rejection. Honoring our acceptability allows us to seek what we desire without fear of consequence or harm, but those who have experienced shame and emotional injury may have lost the sense of "acceptability." Many of us have grown up in the shadows of brokenness. Whether this brokenness taught us that we were not enough to be acceptable or that we were perfect and had to maintain that perfection, the brokenness nurtured an internal dialogue. The messages of shame and rejection eat away at the soul's sense of freedom and acceptance. These messages create a hunger to be "good enough" or "better" in order to be loved. Working to be accepted is just as harmful as resigning to the belief that we could never be acceptable; it's just another shade of shame. Ultimate freedom of our soul, at least in this earthly existence, is found in knowing that we are valued just as we are. One of my congregants said it to me this way: "I love you for no reason at all. I love you just 'cause you is." How humbling to understand that our presence and authenticity are lovable without any pretense or function to compensate. Receiving that freedom is one of the great gifts of God. It takes a special kind of love and a special kind of faith to trust in love without an agenda. I have been blessed to meet this love in life and I do my best to foster that type of self-esteem for those I support in ministry.

We assess this portion of identity by listening and observing the individual being assessed; we learn from listening to how frequently someone asserts their own opinion in a conversation, or how often the person asks for something they need without invitation from someone else. It is also important to pay attention to the nonverbal communication from the person being evaluated. Persons trapped by internal shame, contorting themselves to find a place of belonging, often spend more time looking at the floor or ceiling than at the eyes of the people around them. They will also likely slouch or slump their shoulders in order to minimize their physical presence in social settings.

Connection to the community that we love, the world we engage all around us, provides reinforcement for the freedom found in self-acceptance. In the midst of our acceptability, trusting that we belong and are wanted inspires the element of joy within our human experience. It is a motivation to contribute to the community at large and recognize the investment of others as they contribute to our well-being. Knowing we are loved and lovable is an essential part of spiritual well-being; therein lays our joy.

Connection with
Others or
Community

JOY

Being your most authentic "self" and
being welcomed into connection with a
community as a valued, precious member.

There is joy in knowing that we do not walk this journey alone. There is joy in knowing that someone would note our presence or our absence. Human beings need tangible connection to others. I have met so many people who had every reason and every right to cling to their distrust of people due to their history of abuses or neglect, but those people still tried. I see incredible beauty as I watch the emotionally wounded reaching out to continue finding hearts to draw into their circle of care. I am inspired by their courage, even though parts of my journey have led me to shy away from too many emotional connections with people.

I grew up in a culture that did not have much regard for empowered, outspoken women. I learned quite young to be quiet and contort myself into acceptability. I could adapt to this culture externally, but I craved freedom and authentic acceptance. On my journey to becoming the woman I am today, I never forgot the isolation caused by everything I was—and everything I was not. These experiences were an essential motivation to do the work I do in offering spiritual support. I find incredible joy supporting individuals who lean into new relationships with the fullness of their identity, without apology. I learn from their courage.

God,
a Higher Power,
or a Greater
Whole

PEACE

Trusting in your innate value and the
important, precious purpose of your life.

Connection to God, or a higher power, is also essential to maintaining spiritual well-being. Though the language and perception may differ across cultures, understanding that we are part of something greater is essential to finding our place in a disordered world. Peace comes from understanding that we are only part of something so much greater, but we are most definitely a part. In moments of overwhelming sorrow and pain, we find at least some comfort in knowing that the world is bigger than our present suffering.

In most psychological models of development, finding a contribution we can make to the "whole" is one of the final stages in self-actualization or maturity. Whether creating a legacy within our vocational field, building a family to continue our line, or sharing our wisdom with a future generation, we find our ultimate meaning through trusting that we have changed the world for good.

To have freedom, joy, and peace, we must fully realize our relationship to self, community, and God; these relationships all rest on *connection*. When freedom, joy, and peace are balanced in a healthy individual, their dynamic interactions and experiences with others provide opportunity for balancing and re-balancing of the elements for those with whom they are connected.

When teaching about connection, I refer to it as a "fourth dimension" beyond time, space, and identity. The fourth dimension encompasses the investment of God present within each creature. God's investment intermingles within each individual, each community, and every force of Good that is a part of our world. In my definitions of spiritual care, I attribute this fourth dimension to the work of the Holy Spirit.

In this sense, the relational spirituality concept can assess the healthful function of groups as well. In the introduction, I wrote an analogy of connection using the existence of harmony in the musical world. Just as the musical notes within a chord of sound creates a uniquely beautiful harmony, human beings living out their lives in balanced connection to their own identity, the people that matter most to them, and the God who created them is a uniquely beautiful means of revelation to a finite world. God speaks truth, with and without words, through human experience.

Chapter 4

NOW TO CHANGE THE WORLD

In the preceding chapter, I described some key differences between good leaders and great leaders. Once we change our perception of relational connection, once we recognize the significance of giving and receiving care, we are able to come to a place of greater spiritual well-being. Once we have discovered the sanctity of connection, we have become good spiritual leaders. Recognizing the sanctity of connection means we must recognize the significance of well-being for those around us. To become great spiritual leaders, we must share what we know and be intentional about helping others find a different way of experiencing their world too. The culmination of recognizing the full value of each soul creates momentum for a cultural shift.

In the midst of addressing culture, it is important to evaluate our role in the culture we are attempting to change. It is different in every circumstance and relies on variables that are tightly bound by context. In the work of changing our family, simple conversations or chosen actions can shift culture. A dramatic cultural shift can take place when family members refuse to use words that tear people down. In our home, we do not say "hate'" when referring to other human beings (or dogs, as the case may be—our puppy is a bit trying at times). We do not call people stupid or tell them to shut up. These are important elements of how my husband and I have chosen to raise our children. We value people, and we understand the tremendous weight our words have on others and in the way we relate with each other.

It is necessary to take a less direct, more humble position when attempting to change a vocational environment, even if it is a ministry.

I have described the changes that took place at Hickory Ridge and how those happened, but I did not describe the steps that led up to my ability to create dialogue with both direct support staff and corporate executives. It required significant patience, awareness of the organizational hierarchy, and diplomacy when identifying the areas in need of growth. The closest language I have to describe this dance is that of "code switching." Code switching is a term that describes how someone switches their communication style based on their current cultural context. For example, if you grew up with a marked regional accent or speaking pattern and then lived in a very different region or cultural context, you would alternate your communication style as you move between the two contexts. For me, the language I used when engaging the direct support staff at Hickory Ridge was similar to the interactions I had with my family of origin and my rural relatives because this familiar language mirrored that of the staff.

Hickory Ridge is in a rural area, and the values of that culture are vastly different from those in the corporate offices in the affluent suburbs of Louisville, Kentucky. I know they are different because I was raised on the family farm and made my way to the big city to experience a world larger than any I had known before. The function and perception of relationships in suburban life are very different from those of rural life. The connections in the city are less permanent. In rural life, even if people are no longer on the farm, there is necessary to trust and rely on your neighbors. You don't have to like your neighbors, but you depend on them and they depend on you. In suburban life, relationships are more casual and are built on shared experiences and similar interests. It is much more common to have casual friends and acquaintances in suburban life and simply disconnect from individuals you do not like. Many suburban relationships are mostly about socializing and emotional support; rural relationships are more often based on physical support and trust.

In bridging the gap of language and perception in an organizational structure, it is important to be aware of your own bias. I tend to feel intimidated when engaging suburban or affluent cultures because they are not nearly as familiar to me as the raw, direct interactions that have been a part of my culture since childhood. Over time I have learned to recognize the benefit of politeness and of filtering information. Intricacies of politics and social undertones are important to maintain a thoroughly structured communication train that flows from a corporate office. This type of communication is intended to maintain clear, concise focus for organizations as a whole. I see the difference in relational permanence played out in the relationships of corporate politics; this is how donors and customers approach their interaction with any type of corporate entity. It is necessary to preserve this type of culture in communication because protecting the funding stream is a part of survival in a system held together by financial and bureaucratic balance.

When I am helping to bridge the gap of communication between the corporate culture of company executives and the rural culture of our direct support staff, I have to be careful not to disparage either side. When bridging the gap, build on the commonalities and the singular focus. In churches, no matter what the particular denominational allegiance, the service of God should stand above all else. If there is a problem with that consensus, then the members of the dialogue will find the real heart of the conflict they are facing. In conversations between supportive agencies, the work of the direct care staff is more important than the work of the administrative line, but neither can exist without the other. In a framework of Relational Spirituality, there is no room for social hierarchy. Administrative hierarchy is in place for order, but there is a respectful regard for every human being who is part of an organization. Respect and care cannot survive in relationships if they only flow from one direction.

One of the counterintuitive portions of a Relational Spirituality design is that a program cannot exist in a system that has not adopted the mindset of equal value as an overarching approach to all relationships. Using a cultural view that values all lives as equal cannot exclude anyone within the corporate entity. The respect and consideration of custodial staff, for example, need to be equal to that of executives. Without consensus that the concept of equal value applies to all, the program will quickly succumb to antiquated methods of claiming authority. When I was a child, my father said, "Anybody that has to tell you to respect them probably ain't got what it takes to earn the respect they want."

My father was not right about everything, but he was certainly right about this. Whatever the context, people earn authority by demonstrating their integrity and expertise. Respect can be demanded through policy or submission, but without the integrity to deserve such respect, these efforts only breed resentment. A culture of equality in innate value can only be sustained through authentic appreciation of every contributing member of a community. Whether the members agree or not, whether there is a possible resolution to conflicts or not, the standard of recognizing the value of each person must be absolute.

How do we demonstrate that we value each person and thus build the requisite trust? We demonstrate appreciation and build trust through tangible connections: shaking a hand, helping to complete a menial task, or offering sincere gratitude verbally with sincerity and direct eye contact. All of these will mean more to employees than a note on preprinted stationery from the corporate office. See a person, touch your palm to the palm of another person, and recognize the connection.

My life is changed, and the communities in which I ministered are changed because we have adopted this type of perspective in building our relationships. I will offer a caution, though: it is also important to protect energy and boundaries in the practice of Relational Spirituality. Building authentic relationships carries a proclivity toward deep, emotional attachment that may call us toward seeking or giving more support that is appropriate or healthy. To safeguard each member of the community, it is important to identify and monitor the relationships in our lives. This balance is tenuous for ministers because of the abstract nature of the care we provide. In my life, the only rules I have are related to a method of defining priorities of my time and energy. My family, my husband and children, get first dibs on my energy. Second, I support my closest friends, those who are always there for me through trials and struggles. Third, I claim the time I need for quiet and meditation each day so that I can uphold my strength for the journey. After these dedicated relationships are nurtured, I offer my strength to living out the calling God has placed on my life. In my case, this frequently crosses into the realm of self-care because my soul is fed through the work and revelation in my ministry. I relish the chance to watch others grow in their faith and receive wisdom that helps me do the same. The priorities are not stagnant either. Relationships will need more or less as the requirements of our lives ebb and flow. The ranking is not the point of my caution; recognizing the limitations of our strength and energy is the point. We serve an almighty God. We will never be a god, nor should we attempt to become one.

The realization that our connections are rooted in both the spiritual and the tangible worlds should be daunting; we human beings are a messy, disordered bunch. It is important to realize the limits of our efforts in this process too. Our efforts will be given and received in the midst of the unpredictable existence of us all, meeting with smiles one day and outrage the next. I chalk this variance up to a part of the human condition. All we can really alter is the way we attempt to live out our spiritual growth. There is no stagnation in the movement of the Holy Spirit; we should expect that there will be no stagnation in the experience and revelation that comes through human relationships. To this end, it is important to notice that the work of growing will never be complete. Attempting to change culture, attempting to change ourselves, these are not tasks with finite outcomes. The struggle will continue all of our lives, as part of the maturation of our souls. Take care to notice the victories along the way. Praise the God you love when you see someone you care about making choices that help them find their strength without exploiting the weakness of someone else. Give thanks when you see a community that was estranged find a purpose or task that draws them together for the good of the bigger picture. And feel the relief from a portion of your burden when someone you have mentored teaches the precious truth of human value to the next generation. When you see your student become someone else's mentor, find a grateful consolation in knowing you have been a great leader who walks in the likeness of Christ.

Chapter 5

CONCLUDING THE CLINICAL DISCUSSION

The outcomes of my studies and research in the field of pastoral care offer a great deal of hope surrounding the future possibilities of Relational Spirituality within the context of caring, supportive professions. These vocational areas are the calling of many people who find fulfillment in offering compassion and empathy for the good of others. Recognizing the human soul in the midst of caring relationships provides an avenue for incorporating faith practice into cultures that have not always been embraced by the conservative groups of Judeo-Christian religiosity. While I uphold these traditions as invaluable to my identity and survival in this world, I am sensitive to the distance or indifference of others who have not had my faith experience. The relational approach to spiritual support offers a bridge for different perspectives that highlights a common sense of connection to the people offering and receiving care.

Spirituality is an invaluable area that needs support; our souls demand nurture though the method of communication may not always be clear. The world's labels for the vast cognitive and emotional variations among us make no difference in our souls, and God's love for us isn't predicated on our capacity to be "productive members of society." Recognizing the Divine Investment within every person, the energy spilled out of an Almighty Creator in the birthing of every soul, draws us closer to the heart of God. Recognizing and nurturing souls is the work of good, the work of God, in our tangible realm of existence. Outside of the calling toward a more healthful engagement of humanity, this type of relational spirituality may benefit the cultural climate on many different levels.

Relational Spirituality provides a synergy within functional systems of employees. Means and methods of cooperation increase. Members of communities relate with each other, and agencies also collaborate. The relationships formed within the care setting may then be amplified in the network of systems that work together to provide the ultimate goal of support. Support from area churches, ministries, and nonprofit agencies combine to provide activities and relationships that no entity is capable of providing on its own.

In these situations, the Relational Spirituality model demonstrates the presence of the Spirit within the balance of strengths and weaknesses of organizations. This is the presence of the holy in the support of God's children who are created for one another. This idea is a large part of why the initiative began. The people living at Hickory Ridge offered direction to a greater understanding of spiritual well-being. My journey to communicate the spiritual wisdom they have given me was the origin of this text. My goal has been to convey the culmination of connections that they have helped us all see through their lives and passion.

Where do we go from here? What may be present that was not present before? I pray there is new clarity, a blueprint for the application of a different way of implementing spiritual care. Whatever the setting, whatever the circumstance, the point at which two souls connect holds a sacred truth that can be life-changing if they allow themselves the vulnerability to engage, to make the connection in a given moment.

The overarching goal of this work is to offer an invitation to see a new structure for pastoral and spiritual support. Creating a structure for a Relational Spirituality scaffold in pastoral care makes possible a more healthful model of support that validates individuality as well as unity. A Relational Spirituality model is one that empowers every participant to give and receive care in the context of professional ministry. Furthermore, it is a bridge-building scaffold for this generation. The dialogue of Christianity needs a vernacular that can reveal common ground between our faith tradition and the traditions of those who have different systems of belief. While this model of spiritual care does muddy the boundaries necessary to providing pastoral support by requiring a deeper reciprocity of emotional investment, it also facilitates an authentic attachment that is more akin to the teaching and support offered by Jesus. Internal awareness, not a façade of impenetrable piety, is what maintains our professional identity.

At this point in my ministry, in my life, I understand why we kneel to pray. Submission to a calling is not a process of being raised to any distinguishable height in our time here in this life. It is a process of becoming who we were made to become. Great fear walks alongside us in the journey of becoming. Then again, great fear also exists in the darkness of never dreaming of something more. The difference is that one of these fears strengthens us to hope; the other slowly convinces us that hope is a waste of time. The freedom found in engaging the sacred within ourselves and within others is fuel for hope. It also helps us understand that hope may be rooted in a future that does not involve our happiness, wholeness, or even survival. Hope is a greater thing, a Divine thing that is enlivened when we seek it for those we love and for those we hate. Hope is rooted in the faith that God is present in all things, in all circumstances, and that we are welcomed as companions and co-creators along the way. Sometimes the value of hope is only that we question a possibility too daunting to imagine for a future we may never see. That is the beauty of understanding God alive in relationships: we see hope in the very breath of us all.

Unexpected Revelations

Relational Spirituality has sparked a dialogue that may help to build a means of quality assurance for Hickory Ridge's program structure. The training at the heart of this spiritual support program was the first step in the formal implementation of programming I worked to develop over five years. Early on, data from Hickory Ridge showed very encouraging results.

First, data collected after the informal implementation of the Relational Spirituality approach indicated an increase in adaptive function—the way those we support engage their world. Across the population of Hickory Ridge, adaptive function scores increased with a range of 2 percent to 48 percent over a twenty-four-month period. That is an impressive change.

A second outcome of this type of spiritual life programming has been the deepened emotional investment of the employees who are part of our system. Many have expressed their gratitude for the tools gained in spiritual life assessments. The process of discovering the life stories of individuals we support provides a stronger basis for interpersonal connection. The cues surrounding the nonverbal communications and personal preferences allow for meaningful communications to take place earlier in caring relation-ships. This depth of relational connection helps improve the emotional feedback caregivers receive because they can discern what others may not be able to speak in words. Theory would suggest that the reciprocity of relationship necessary for this model of care would, in turn, foster spiritual well-being in the direct care staff, which would likely contribute to job satisfaction. It would also increase performance in caring professions, as job performance is based on the quality of life of those supported. Administrative and corporate professionals would gladly participate in outcomes that further these objectives in their workplace, whether pastoral care is of primary interest or not.

Another outcome of this project surrounds the interconnectedness of the human race and has most profoundly changed my own outlook. When I began my doctoral adventure three years ago, I did so with some reluctance and some relief. We had entered new territory at Hickory Ridge. We were attempting to implement a new way of providing spiritual support, particularly for people whose disabilities and sensory defenses had never allowed them to participate in traditional congregational worship. I struggled to put the elements of nurturing a human spirit on paper at all, much less submit these "objectives" for approval or denial in light of state and federal regulations. I hoped that working through the dialogue and concepts toward the doctor of ministry in Christian spirituality would help me find the words to express an intuitive awareness that was part of my natural way of relating to people.

The outcome is much more complex than I anticipated three years ago. I entered into this professional growth to learn how I might teach the skill of seeing the beautiful spirits of those we supported at Hickory Ridge, a skill I learned from watching the seasoned, loving caregivers I worked alongside every day and who worked tirelessly to support the residents.

I will continue the work of dialogue and caring in the name of God. I will offer what I am able in further developing the concept of nurturing spirituality through tangible care in our world; this is the calling of Christ, who said, "As much as you have done it to the least of these, you have done it to me" (Matt 5:40, CEV). We are each the least of these in tandem, our strengths and weakness intermingled in life's journey. None are absent of giftedness. None are without the capacity to change my life or yours; the most profound and beautiful change can be found in places we never expect.

As I finish writing this text, I still find balancing the programming structure and cultural change daunting. The task is not so centered on proving my competence as it was in the beginning of this journey toward spiritual education. That goal was a camouflaging mask, something that drew out my inmost being through this process of growth. Through this journey, I have learned from beautiful souls who have invited me to see myself and others with the eyes of God, to slow down and hear a truth that words cannot speak. I will teach others to see the beauty of the Spirit within us all because that is the gift I have been given by those I love at Hickory Ridge. The responsibility of this gift is the same as the responsibility attached to any gift offered out of love: we are responsible to teach its value and to pay it forward.

Part 2

Bridging the Gap from Head to Heart

WHERE CLINICAL THEORY AND LIVED EXPERIENCE MEET

The second section of this book may seem like a divergence from the work of Relational Spirituality, but I assure you it is not. After reading through the clinical portion of this text, I realized I had included a lot of information but not much of my own story. Part of what I relay here is the story of revelations that came to me within and through the lives of those I support in ministry. My story is not drastically different from that of many others. It is a story of cultural shifts, transformation, and a spirit shaped by the care invested by souls that did not have to make that choice. I am a product of the embodied experience of a faith verified through the tangible relationships I have encountered in this world. I pray that I pay the care, guidance, and motivation forward to those I meet in this life, at least more often than not. The following chapters are vignettes from my life. Most of the stories are focused on the work of the Spirit in my career in chaplaincy, but a few of the stories are about the parts of my life that led me toward ministry.

I hope that the concepts of integration and growth are evident in the stories I am sharing. I hope they also speak to the reciprocal nature of spiritual revelation. The Holy Spirit does not move in one direction at a time because we say so. The Holy Spirit moves through and toward each soul in the context of relationships, so the revelation is available to each member who participates in relational encounters.

There are questions at the conclusion of the following chapters to provide space and time for each reader's consideration. This part of the book is intended to help you examine spirituality in an abstract and open way. Recognizing the intentional vulnerability and engagement that are nurtured when soul meets soul is an essential part of spiritual growth.

We truly are members of one another, as stated in Christian Scripture. Every developmental theory defines connection and relationship as key components of the shape taken on by each life. We were made to need one another; we were made to accept that need and be courageous enough to participate in our own formation and that of the people we allow within the confines of our most vulnerable places. This exchange is the major foundation of the human spirit, fragile enough to be injured by a disapproving glance, resilient enough to thrive despite unimaginable trauma; it is the truest gift of the human experience.

Chapter 1

MY POINTS OF INTERSECTION

The prospect of sharing stories from my life creates a terror I cannot adequately describe. I am a private woman, proud, and awkward to exceptional proportions. However, Relational Spirituality requires we recognize the intersections of our story with the stories of those we support throughout our ministry. Maintaining a constant awareness of our spiritual and emotional presence is essential to the work of meeting another human being's soul in relationship. We can easily encounter others, even live out compassion and empathy, without a mindful attendance to the soul. However, we cannot facilitate or experience lasting change if we have not found the capacity to hold appropriate respect for the Divine Investment within ourselves and within those who celebrate and ache in front of us. I am quite aware of this truth; it has been made clear to me repeatedly throughout my life. So I am writing down my vulnerability despite my fear. In my life of faith, I have adopted a mantra that has helped me crawl out of a cocoon that held me captive for much of my young adult life: it is a sin to cower once we know better. And thus here is my story of coming to faith, my offering of some perspective surrounding the brokenness that brought me to be sensitive to the beautiful truth conveyed to me through some exceptional souls.

I was raised outside of Danville, Kentucky. My parents were both teachers, the first in their families to attend college. They met during their studies at Berea College and went on to live with a dedication to paying forward the gifts of education and care that brought them lives easier than the ones in which they were born. My parents taught my brother, my sister, and I that our gifts of talent and intellect were a responsibility to something bigger than ourselves. We learned to work hard from the time we were young and made our education a priority, but we also contributed to the work of our family farm. My father lived out the dreams of his father and grandfather and great-grandfather as he raised much of the food our family ate and taught others to do the same.

My mother taught elementary physical education. She had loved sports throughout her childhood and built a vocation on that love. She relished the freedom she got from playing and teaching children to play. She loved watching the wonder in the eyes of the smallest of her students and nurturing the character of the oldest. My mother is a creative, compassionate, and tender soul. She emits her passion through every cell of her being.

Despite the obvious love my parents had for one another, the ghosts of their impoverished upbringings frequently caused confusion and chaos in the early years of my life. I was torn between the structure of my father's logic and the untethered spirit of my mother's creativity. I loved and respected them both, but I hated to watch those two passions meet head to head in our living room. My brother, seven years older than I, would frequently scoop me up and sit in our bedroom closet with me in the midst of some of the more heated exchanges. We would eat dry Kool-Aid out of the package and play with his Star Wars figures until the yelling died down. Because he loved me through my fear, my brother taught me that I was strong enough to survive just about any storm.

My baby sister, three years younger than I, did not need the same security. As she grew, she always wanted to be in the midst of the storm and fight against it, trying to solve things or draw the heat of the fire. I still appreciate her desire to fight or to solve, but for me, getting in harm's way seemed like a hopeless risk. It wasn't until I had children of my own that I appreciated engaging in a battle for the sake of those who would come after me.

In our home, we all knew we were loved because of our parents' desperate loyalty and drive. They fought for us and for a better world around us. We had all the tangible things we could ever need. We all worked. We were responsible to and for one another. We sweat and struggled and did everything we could with every resource at our disposal. In that life, my father taught me to pay attention to the world around me in order to protect myself and the animals in my care. I learned to "listen with my eyes," as he said. He taught me to listen to what the animals were speaking to me with their gestures, their posture, and the unspoken loyalty that shined through the eyes of those creatures that counted on me for their very survival. It was the method of teaching passed through the generations of his family, with origins in the Cherokee tradition of his family. We were taught to recognize that every life was something made by God; people, animals, plants, and the whole of creation had a sacred element to be honored. We were taught to show respect to God's work by attending to its care. This facet of our family culture, the theology I inherited, is still at the core of my theological perspectives today.

In the midst of our culture of being responsible and devoting our full strength to the work of God, I somehow lost the truth of my own value. I forgot to recognize myself as something God made and loved. I forgot I was valuable outside of all that I could do. I worked so diligently that I became the sweat of my brow and the products of my labor. I was not the only soul lost in our all-consuming busyness.

When I was eight years old, my mother suffered a significant bout of depression that nearly took her from our family. I remember seeing her as a mighty tower that had begun to crumble, a broken woman on the floor with streams of sorrow flowing from her. I knew her tender heart because it had given birth to mine. I ached for all that I saw her losing. I could *do* nothing to fix or stop her pain. The scariest part of the day she crumbled was looking into the eyes of my strong father and seeing his terror. He could not fix it either. That day I learned the frailty of us all.

During the first days of my mother's desperate battle with depression, my brother, sister, and I were sent to stay with my mother's family. We were dispersed among her brothers and sisters, as none of them had the time or money to keep all of us. We were supposed to be sheltered in a safe place away from our home. Our parents were working to gather themselves again and find a way forward for us all. However, in that time, when we were already lost and out of touch with everyone, we each experienced excruciating brokenness, abuse, and violence that would change us forever. I thought staring into the eyes of my broken mother would be the greatest experience of powerlessness possible; I was very mistaken.

I am not certain of how much time passed. Without a timeline for returning home, the march of weeks and days became meaningless. I only survived. On the darkest of those days, in the midst of a horrific moment of abuse, I heard a voice within my mind. I believe it to be the voice of God; that voice helped me keep breathing when I no longer wanted to live. That voice said, "Hold on, darlin'. We are gonna make it."

I had read Scripture and known the stories of Old Testament prophets from evenings spent on my grandmother's knee. I knew that God was always surprising people, creating a miraculous somebody out of a person whom much of the world might have looked right past. I did not understand why the voice of God would find someone like me, a little girl who could easily die without many people even noticing, but I was grateful to have been found. I am still grateful. That voice spoke hope into my broken heart and peace into my fearful mind. That voice has been the God I love since that day: Abba, the one who lives and breathes with and through me.

Eventually, I returned home with my brother and my sister in the backseat of my aunt's Buick. The four-hour ride was mostly silent aside from the repeated stops to use the restroom and be sick on the side of mountainous, winding roads. When we walked into our home, it was still the cluttered mess it always had been—farm coats and boots, toys and groceries randomly strewn about. Still, the space helped me breathe better. Though imperfect, home had always been my favorite place to be. My sister and I were bounding in our excitement to be home and see our parents again, but my father quickly stifled our giggles and squeals. He told us to "shut up and calm the hell down." We both stopped. My sister leaned back on me, and I on my brother. We saw our mother lying on the couch, barely awake, with a washrag on her forehead. Her face was drawn and her beautiful eyes that were usually a sparkling swirl of blue, gray, and green like the sea were bloodshot and empty. Where had her sparkle gone? Why was my father so angry? I did not understand. I thought she would be better. I thought everything would be like it used to be. In my fear, I leaned harder into my brother, the person who taught me that having someone to love made the storm bearable. He pushed me forward. "Get off me," he said. He had the same, angry expression as my father, but his chin quivered from tears because he had not yet learned to lock his jaw to stop them. He turned and stomped toward his room. I felt my little sister, just five years old, lean into me again and look up at me. She had the same blue-gray-green eyes of my mother, but hers still had a beautiful sparkle. "Is Mama still sick?"

"Your Mama's not gonna be better for a long time. She feels bad. It's your all's job to help me take care of her and let her rest." This was the answer we got from our father as he gathered our bags from our aunt and pushed us toward our bedroom.

"Put all this away and clean your damn room. It's a mess in there."

We waddled down the hallway with our backpacks full of clothes. Once we got to our room, Dad closed the door and said he would be back in a bit. My little sister looked up at me, her tiny chin dimpling as tears formed in her eyes. I hugged her and told her everything would be okay. I was lying and I knew it. I lied anyway, and then I led her over to our bedroom closet, dragging our backpacks behind us. We cuddled in the corner of that closet, talking about things we could do to help Mama smile again. I did my best to convince myself and my sister that we were going to be fine. I spent many years at that task, without any lasting success.

Once I saw the broken shack our safe fortress of a home had become, I did not dream of making things worse by speaking about any of the things I had endured while we were away from home. I was not certain how to adequately describe what I lived through, and I wasn't certain if those experiences were perpetrated against me or perpetrated because of me. I only knew I felt terrified, unlovable, and filthy. I was tarnished beyond repair, or so I thought.

In the aftermath of that experience, when my home no longer felt like home, I claimed a new sanctuary for my heart in the arms of my father's mother. She was four feet, ten inches of sassy Baptist fire. She was kind and gracious but never faltered in maintaining the integrity of her family. My grandfather had passed away three years before. He had struggled with cancer for a long time, and I have few memories of him. Most of those memories are of helping my grandmother take care of him as he lay dying in their living room. After his passing, my grandmother came around to a different type of freedom. She adored my grandfather, but he was prone to moodiness and yelling like my father. Once his yelling was gone, her house echoed only with peaceful silence, old-lady laughter, and off-key hymn tunes. I came to love the sounds of that house. It was only three-quarters of a mile from our home. When life became too chaotic, I would scoop up my baby sister and we would head down the country road toward the gray stone house.

Her house had hardwood floors and cream-colored walls, and it always smelled of Sunday morning bacon and vanilla fields' perfume. My grandmother's acceptance was something I never doubted; in uncertain times of our life, I craved it as a thread that helped me find my way to survival. I remember toddling down the road in my footed pajamas, with my baby sister in our yellow wagon, searching for peace.

Our grandmother never questioned why we were there, never turned us away, and never failed to provide a sanctuary within her warm, enfolding arms that soothed so much heartache. She made sure we had dinner and celebrated birthdays and drove us to school and church activities. We still had a home with our parents, but we had also had a safe haven when we needed one. I did not understand what a gift I had been given until I was much older; I did not understand how precious that haven was until she died and it was gone. I was immeasurably changed by the love of that tiny, feisty woman. She introduced me to God and nurtured me toward a life of faith. As I grew, the love she modeled blossomed into an enigmatic, unbreakable connection to the God who would always welcome me home into quiet peace and the shelter of loving arms.

I wanted to claim my faith shortly after returning home from the nightmare I had known when I was eight years old. I did not believe I was worthy of the acceptance and grace described by our country pastors in their sermons, but I yearned to become worthy someday. I was also terrified to walk in front of a congregation of people to make my profession.

In our small country church, I was terrified of being seen or heard. The culture of that rural, conservative congregation did not make room for a girl, or woman, to be a prominent figure. Women were expected to serve with quiet grace and follow the instructions they were given. If I was invisible, I was safe. That was the new reality of our home. I worked diligently to stay out of people's way, not to trouble people, not to upset things. I worked very hard at being invisible, but I also worked hard to be seen. I tried to secure as much affirmation and acceptance as possible. It was, and sometimes still is, an impossible paradox created from my own frantic attempts to stay safe and still have some outside validation of my existence.

The day the pastor of our church came to our home when I was eleven years old, I remember being lost in the swirl of that paradox. He came into our house on a Monday when we were off from school. He said he wanted to come and talk to me because he had seen me crying during the sermon the day before. He asked me why I cried. I felt myself choking back tears again as I answered, "You talked about the waters of baptism washing away every bad thing we have ever done. You said the grace of Jesus could cover everything and mend every heartache."

He looked confused but attentive. "I did say that. The Bible says that. You believe the Bible, don't you?"

I searched within myself. I did believe in the Bible; my grandmother had recited Scripture to and with me since I had learned to speak. I valued those words as God's truth, yet I was stuck on what felt impossible about the pastor's words the day before. I looked at him, someone my grandmother had taught me to trust as an active part of my spiritual education and faith. In that moment, I chose to believe in something even though it felt impossible. I chose to accept a truth of my faith even though the emotions within me screamed a different truth. I chose to try. I looked into his intent, puzzled eyes, swallowed my tears so that I could speak, and answered with a declaration that would begin the course toward my own freedom, made possible by the limitless power of the God I loved. I asked him, "So God can love me?"

He looked even more confounded. "Of course God can love you. God loves us all. You are no exception to that."

I swallowed again and spoke my deepest, most vulnerable desire. "I want, more than anything, to be clean. Can God help me feel clean again?"

The baptismal waters I experienced the month following my public profession of faith did not deliver the "cleansing" that I had anticipated; that came much later, after a lot of important work alongside skilled therapists and teachers. With their help, I finally found my freedom from shame. What I did gain from my baptism was a way to seek more for my life than I imagined possible. After all, I was not seeking God's will for the good of myself but to make certain that the life I was living was fully open to the possibilities of the service of God. The difference in those two motivations seemed extraordinary to me during my adolescent years. Now, I see that the God I serve has always wanted my life to be lived joyfully with all of the fullness I can find; the difference is not nearly as vast as I assumed then.

The shame of everything I had lived during the shadows of years of abuse, the responsibility I had taken on for making life harder for my parents, and the guilt I carried over every mistake and bad thought in my head rolled out of me with my sobs. That young pastor had no idea what I was talking about, but he hugged me, dried my tears, and spoke a prayer that initiated a journey of faith that helped me claim meaning for my life. I am not certain if the cleansing waters of God's grace led to my redemption or if I was redeemed by *my choice* to claim God's truth over all else, but I am convinced that the difference between those two things is negligible to the effect on my soul.

What I understand is this: God loves me, even when I deem myself unlovable. God sends ambassadors to shape me, ambassadors to shape us all, throughout this life. I was on the path to healing, whether by the waters of baptism or by a kind word from a trusted representative of God who spoke a truth louder than the lies inside my head. In the midst of a messy, beautiful, heartbreaking, spirit-building journey as an adolescent, I found a way to see myself and this world differently through the care of people who loved me when they did not have to. I believe God is alive in that care. I believe God changed me through that care. And I believe I can pay that gift forward for the glory of a God who has helped me keep breathing when it seemed impossible. That belief is the foundation at the root of my calling to minister. I love in the name of my God, who loved me when I didn't love myself, who found me in my darkest moments of terror, and who has never left me.

Though not all of my story holds so much struggle and sorrow, I share this portion so that I can lay the foundations for the revelation I have found in the work I do alongside adults with IDD. I see them as precious because I was raised to see the sanctity in every life, seeing the "light" of every soul as instructed by my grandmother. I try to listen with all of myself as I *pay attention to the world around me.* I nurture people toward their freedom because I was nurtured toward my own. I recognize many who are nearly invisible because I have been "no one" and I have been "nothing"—or so I thought. I have been formed by my relationships. For good or for ill, I evaluated those who entered into my world and my heart. I did my best to adopt the pieces that resembled the woman I wanted to become, and I lived in opposition to the pieces that separated me from that identity. I continue this journey, as we all do, because the process of "becoming" is not something we finish. Since God deemed loneliness the first thing in all of creation that was "not good," human beings have been changed by knowing and being known by one another. The sacred is alive in this world. We are changed when we allow ourselves the opportunity to feel, to care, and to engage the sanctity that lives through and around every soul.

Questions for the Soul

1. Do you deem yourself worthy of love? Why?

2. What brokenness has built your greatest strength?

3. How do you choose to invest the energy of your anger?

Chapter 2

THE FIRST TIME I MET DEATH

I am a female ordained Baptist minister. From those identifiers, you may be able to gather that I am not what many people think of as a "typical woman." When I speak casually about myself, I say that I am a freak—but a charming one. I have always felt outside of things, just a little different or odd. On her good days, my mother would say, "Pay no mind to what people say. God just made you a little uni-Q [pronounced "you-nee-cue"] and there ain't no harm in that." I took that as an affirmation of my weirdness and chose to believe I would be special someday. The irony is that I have had a few "someday" moments in my lifetime but a lot more "what the hell" days than I can count. Through each type of day, I learned to believe in the truth that my mother told me: I was made to be different. Learning to cherish that revelation would become my strength in adulthood. In my childhood, though, it was not strength. After my mother lost much of her sparkle to illness and my father's spirit gave way to his frustrations, I desperately sought a place to belong.

As I mentioned in the previous chapter, I found that safe haven at my grandmother's house. I did not know what I needed or wanted in the moments when I gathered up my sister for escape, but I definitely knew what I did not need or want. I knew the way to peace, so I took my sister and we made our way toward it. I recognized my place in leadership as I matured; it was the same feeling I had when I scooped up my baby sister. It also involved the frustration and sore hands of pulling that stupid wagon up a really long gravel hill. I was so angry, but we had not made it to our peace yet, so I kept pulling, and it is that struggle that led me toward a life of ministry. My spirit of leadership was also found in being "uni-Q" just like mother had said.

Oddly, I found a kinship when I began reading more about the disciples and prophets throughout Scripture. Not a single influential figure in the Bible is considered ordinary or average. Every leader in Scripture is a bit freakish in their own right. I figured that if God could use those freakish people to speak a greater truth, then God could use me too. So I stepped into a calling toward ministry when I was still a teenager. The choice was especially gratifying because it contradicted my father's theology that rejected women ministers. Adolescents all rebel in their own way; my way might not have been drinking and breaking curfew, but it was a rebellion nonetheless.

In my journey of ministry, I found some conflict and some celebration, like any minister in the midst of formation, but the perspective that meant the most to me was that of my tiny, blue-eyed grandmother. She had led me toward loving a magnanimous God throughout my entire life. I watched thunderstorms with her from her back porch swing, snuggling into her armpit whenever there was a thunderclap. She would whisper down to me, "See that lightnin' dance. Look how big our God is," as she smiled and pulled me in closer to her soft cushion of protection. I learned to relate the beauty of great things to the identity of God, even if those things scared me.

When I was twelve years old, I spent the night with a friend, Julie. She took me to church with her family on the following Sunday, and I was astonished at who I saw preaching from the pulpit that morning. There was a lady preaching! I had never seen a lady preacher in my life; I don't know that I had ever even considered it as a possibility. When I got home that afternoon, I called my grandmother with a lot of excitement. She giggled to hear me talk about the "lady preacher" I had seen. The woman who delivered the sermon that day was a friend of hers, Rev. Jo Garnett. She was excited to hear that I had the chance to meet someone she admired so much. The following Sunday, I couldn't help sharing my excitement with the members of the little country church who had raised me in faith since my birth. I shared the exciting discovery with the head of the deacons, who also happened to have been my Sunday school teacher for as long as I could remember. He was a kind old man with sparkling white hair and bright blue eyes. He had bounced me on his knee, helped me memorize Bible Drill verses, and taught me to proclaim the gospel of Jesus with everything I had. I hoped he would find the same excitement with my discovery that I had, but I could tell from his gruff expression that he was not pleased. I was thoroughly confused by his lack of enthusiasm. Didn't he understand how awesome my discovery was?

He continued to scowl and puffed his chest as he began to speak. "A woman has no place at a pulpit."

Again, I was confused by his words. I looked at him with puzzlement, so he continued. "A woman preaching at the head of a congregation is heresy." I knew that word. Heresy was something that he loved to include in our early theological training. His statement confounded me even further.

"Mr. Lawson, you have told me my whole life that I am supposed to share the gospel of Jesus. Why would it matter where I stand when I'm doing it?"

His eyes got big and he pursed his lips. I knew that look. He made that face when I hit his white Buick with a baseball one Sunday afternoon. He was furious. He closed his big eyes, turned his face to the ground, and walked away without a word.

I quickly found my grandmother and told her what had happened. I honestly did not understand why he was so upset with me. My chin had fallen to my chest along with my tears, so she lifted my face so that my eyes could meet hers as she spoke.

"It's okay, baby. You didn't do anything at all. Some people are just strange about things. I do believe this church has decided who they are gonna be, and I don't think we can be here with them anymore. Ain't no harm in choosin' different, but that don't mean it doesn't hurt. I'm sorry."

I felt the reassurance she offered as a soothing balm to the swirl of hurt and confusion, but I did not understand why people could not stay in the same place and believe different things. Twenty years later, with my profession rooted in the practice and nurture of faith, I still don't understand why we cannot seem to honor one another despite our differences.

The next Sunday came, and my grandmother dressed herself to the nines, helping me to do the same. We were going to the city church where I had seen a woman minister for the first time. Bear in mind that this city church had about three hundred members in contrast to the thirty members filling the pew of the country church where I had been raised. She drove into the large parking lot and walked me into the church through the monstrous white pillars that upheld a massive church roof, topped with a bell tower. I felt very small as I entered the sanctuary adorned with crystal chandeliers, organ pipes, and oak crown molding. But I found more acceptance and spiritual guidance in that congregation than I had ever known in the smaller church. Alongside my grandmother, I learned that God was big enough to hold my questioning and love for me. I learned to seek and to guide, no matter how ill equipped I may have felt. And I watched my grandmother delight in every discovery I made along the way.

It was shortly after I was married, just as I was finishing my undergraduate degree in music at the University of Louisville, that my grandmother fell ill. She had struggled with rheumatoid arthritis for as long as I could remember, but this time the disease had pressed her past the point of recovery. During this battle, I found myself sitting by her hospital bed with my husband, reading portions of the *Herald Leader* to her while she tried to stay awake. I flipped the page over and saw the classified ads. I was excited to see them. I have always gotten excited about bargain, secondhand furniture that I can repair. That day there was nothing in the furniture section for me to dream about, but there was a small ad for a new Baptist seminary that was accepting students. I kind of laughed and said with no real fire behind it, "Maybe someday I can go to seminary and figure out how to be a good minister."

I did not have faith in anything at that point. The matriarch who held our family's universe on its axis lay beside me dying, and all I could do was read her the newspaper and try to pretend I wasn't terrified. I did not trust in my calling. I did not trust in my judgment. I still trusted in my God, but there were days when I questioned even that.

In her typical fashion, the mighty, four-foot-tall woman smiled a sideways grin and spoke softly. "What are you waiting for, baby?"

Even as she lay dying, she offered an invitation for me to walk in courage. She had been that voice throughout my entire life. Much of my identity was tangled within the strands of my grandmother's influence. I applied for seminary that night. I wasn't sure how everything would work out in my future, how I would afford the education, how I would find a place to minister, or anything else.

She simply asked what I was waiting for, and I decided that waiting because I was afraid was not a good reason to wait. I chose to try to mimic my grandmother by living into my own faith the way I had witnessed her living into hers. Granny would study her Bible every morning at her kitchen table, sipping coffee and watching the birds dance around the bird feeder outside her kitchen window. I remember seeing her sit and read her ragged Bible until the sun shone through that window at sunrise, like God smiling a bright "hello" to her in their morning meeting. I was still little, and I would pull up a chair beside her, drinking chocolate milk instead of coffee. She generally read me passages from the Psalter during these morning meetings. She told me that the Psalms were meant to be our anchor. She said they were mostly short and something to remember when we couldn't remember anything else. "Even Jesus quoted the Psalms in his darkest hour," she said. When I think of keeping the word of God ever on my lips, I remember the wisdom of my grandmother. The Psalter was so woven into my mind and heart that it would appear in moments when nothing else stayed tethered to my train of thought.

I received word that I had been accepted into seminary as my grandmother grew weaker. Her failing organs robbed her of the ability to stay coherent and present when I was with her, and she forgot who I was most days. I stayed anyway. I was afraid, but I was pretending to be brave. I was brave as I fed her. I was brave as I tried to help her do her physical therapy. I was even brave when I changed her diapers. As I drove home after spending days caring for her, I did not feel brave. I did not feel strong. I only felt pain and disorientation. I raged at the God I love. At first I raged about the illness that had come like a thief, moving with a vicious speed that stole my grandmother's independence, her happiness, and her mind. Then I raged at my God for letting that thief have her for so long. I wanted her to have peace. She deserved peace.

"God, please let her die." This was my guilt-ridden prayer over and over through the days of watching her struggle at the end.

And then the day came when my prayer was answered. My husband and I received the phone call that she was dying and we needed to get to the hospital immediately. We traveled eighty-seven miles in just over thirty minutes. I ran down the hospital hallway to find her in a darkened room, attached to an octopus of medical equipment buzzing and beeping through the frantic white noise in my head. A nurse was anxiously circling her bed, administering medications and trying to stop the tiny streams of blood that were flowing out of every IV port she had.

I just stood and watched for a few moments, waiting to wake up or feel like I was actually part of the reality that was in front of me. There it was. I finally caught my breath and balance. I put my hand on the nurse's shoulder and asked her to stop.

"Please, she has fought long enough. Please, just let her rest."

The nurse's eyes were already filled with tears, and my words seem to help them flow. She nodded and made her way to my uncle, who was standing in the doorway of the hospital room. Then she returned and began removing the tentacles of the medical machine octopus from the little old woman I loved so dearly. I was happy to see her face look like her face again. I was grateful that she was going to rest. I was grateful to be there beside her.

In the last moments of my Granny's life, when most others had left the room where she lay dying, I knelt by her bed, brushing her hair, humming "Amazing Grace," and reciting Psalm 23 over and over for three hours. She was right in the wisdom of keeping myself grounded through the knowledge of God, even when it felt like my entire world would crumble beneath my feet.

"Though I walk through the valley of the shadow of death, I will fear no evil, for Thou are with me . . ."

She breathed her last, and for a moment—just a moment—I forgot how to breathe too. The world should have stopped spinning. Everything and everyone should have stopped breathing too. How would this world go on without the person who helped me believe that my life was meant for something good? How would I go on without the person who held the messy family of my childhood together?

"I will fear no evil . . ."

"Be strong in the Lord . . ."

Then the desperate hunger for air finally took center stage in my focus. I gasped in the air of an entirely new existence because something inside me, something innately present in my physical self, had pressed my desperation to keep living. I inhaled the breath of the new world.

I chose to keep breathing, though I didn't know what that choice would mean. My husband, my dearest friend, stood alongside me as I tried to uncover what it would be to exist now, without my Granny. His tears flowed just as steadily as mine did. He loved the feisty, joyful, righteous woman too, but his heart also broke for my hurt.

He helped me up from my kneeling position, both of my legs asleep from holding the position for hours as I waited for my world to end. He lifted my chin so that my eyes met his, tears flowing steadily down both our faces. He nodded his head and gave me a painful smile. He didn't use words; we didn't need them. His pained smile and nod spoke the truth of the moment: "We survive. You and me. We will survive this." I was so grateful for the connection to such a sweet, tender, and unbreakable love. He pulled me into a hug and placed his hand on the back of my head as people do when they are sheltering a fragile infant or child. I buried my head and forgot I was an adult. I forgot the façade of an unwavering faith. I simply fell to pieces in his embrace and allowed my world to crumble. It was all right to fall to pieces; my husband Chip was holding the world on its axis so I didn't have to.

Prior to my grandmother's death, I did not know that something that did not threaten my physical survival could terrify me so deeply. I did not understand that I could be both happy for her relief and also broken from the loss of someone who was so essential in how I defined myself. That moment of powerlessness taught me something about beauty. That day, I recognized the necessity of a God who would never depart from us or leave us in our heartache.

The day I met death was the day that I lost my grandmother. It was the day that I understood the beauty of death; I knew there were some circumstances in which death was a kindness. It was also the day I recognized the need for chaplains and pastors in hospitals. I relive that moment whenever I sit alongside families who are losing someone they love. I may or may not externalize any of my memories, but they are always with me. Clinically, this could be seen as an informed, empathetic presence. It could also be seen as a lack of focus on the family I am present to serve. There is a central focus on the present moment—an awareness of and connection to the souls who ache right in front of us. But it also includes a haunting echo of the heartache we have endured and now redeem as we choose to serve others through the wisdom gained from our own experience.

I believe the moments of my desperation teach me to strive for humility in the sacred space of sitting alongside others who are losing someone they love. There are moments in life that hold us in the wise lap of powerlessness, like children listening to a truth from a trusted elder. We feel small, we know the limitations of our fragile being, and we learn a precious truth of perspective. So much of our time is spent wrapped up in the concern of choices and perceptions, and much of that time is wasted trying to wrangle a reality that we will never really control. The awareness that we have very little control over our reality can be terrifying, but it can also be liberating.

Questions for the Soul

1. Who helped you become who you are?

2. How did their influence shape your journey?

3. How do you shape the journeys of others?

Chapter 3

BLACK LACE BAPTISM

When I began my work at Hickory Ridge, I did not imagine that I would have the opportunities to do the work of parish ministry that had been a part of my calling since I was nineteen years old. I thought I would not be able to preach or counsel or perform religious rites like baptisms or weddings. I was terribly mistaken in these assumptions. I have performed many weddings and funerals during my time as the spiritual life coordinator at Hickory Ridge, but I have had the opportunity to perform only one baptism. It was an experience I will never forget. It was a beautiful, clumsy, and hilarious occasion in which my pastoral identity met internal conflict with my feminine self.

Callie, a young woman who was supported by our agency, wanted to be baptized. This young woman was beautiful, inside and out, and I do not believe she had the inclination to do harm to anyone she had ever met. I saw in her a pure soul, but she disagreed with my opinion.

"Our preacher said that people who are baptized go to heaven. My whole family has been baptized, even my little sisters, but my preacher wouldn't let me because he said I didn't understand."

I saw desperation in her eyes. Now I understood why this meant so much to her. She did not trust in the eternity she had been promised without going through the same steps toward redemption that were taken by every other member of her family.

"What do you think will change when you are baptized?" I asked. I wanted to see how much doctrine she had within the context of her family's faith tradition.

"I'm not sure, but I know God is with me and I know I wanna be in heaven with my family someday." Her bright eyes shone with a hopeful expectation.

"Okay. How about you and I sit down and talk this through with your mom and see what we can do to help you understand all the steps that are part of being baptized? We can work through things and then you can decide what you feel like God wants you to do."

"God wants us all to be baptized. He wouldn't leave people behind, not even me."

My heart sank as I heard her words, but I kept my composure so our conversation could continue. "You are absolutely correct. God would never leave you behind, not ever." I explained that God made her soul innocent, a relative truth for many who struggle with the concepts of sin, repentance, and redemption due to the limitations that accompany their disabilities. I offered her a reassuring smile as I spoke. I decided then that we were going to find a way for this young woman to be baptized. If I had to find a country creek to do it, I was going to make certain that she knew that she would spend eternity in heaven with her family and the God who adored her.

Callie and I began working together every week. We made our way through all of the prominent stories of the Old and New Testaments, highlighting the concepts of faith. We talked about the life of Jesus and the basic principles he taught as he showed people how to live a life of righteousness. We talked about the gifts she had been given to care for and about people she met in her life. We spent over six months in the journey toward helping Callie learn to speak of her faith for herself. I had never worked so hard with a congregant who wanted to make a profession. Honestly, I wondered if I had ever known anyone who had such a deep yearning to claim their faith for themselves.

As Callie and I worked on helping her retain the information she chose as vital to her faith, I did the work of finding a community that would welcome her and her family into their congregation. Hickory Ridge is a nonprofit organization with roots in Christian tradition, but it is not a church. I had to find a church for this family to be a part of, one that would welcome my friend and help her continue the faith training we had begun months before.

In conversation with a handful of area ministers, I found a pastor who was led by a compassionate faith toward including any of God's children who wanted to make their profession of faith and become part of his congregation. I was excited to find a community of faith that would greet this family with smiles and open arms. I couldn't wait to call Callie and let her know that we could schedule a time for her to meet with the pastor and make her public profession before she was baptized. Callie looked at me with confusion when I gave her the good news.

"Why do I have to meet with another pastor? You're my pastor, right? You and me spent a long time learning about the Bible so I could be baptized like my sisters."

I smiled. While she didn't understand the logistical parts of this rite that had to be sorted through, for me, that was the most difficult part of the work we were doing. I also felt great pride when she called me her pastor. How funny it was to hear that now. I remembered the conversations I had with my white-haired childhood Sunday school teacher on the day I first professed my excitement about the possibility of a woman becoming a minister. What a journey I had taken from being a naïve, twelve-year-old girl to becoming this young woman's pastor. How was I going to tell her that I could not be her pastor, at least not in the community outside of our programming?

"You see, Callie, it's important that the person who baptizes you be the pastor of the church you and your family are going to attend. It's kind of a rule that the pastor does that kind of stuff so he can welcome you into the community there." I was trying to explain in a way that would help her understand and gain some trust in the new relationship she was going to form.

"I don't know him, though, and I don't know if he knows I am supposed to be baptized."

"He knows you have worked very hard to get to this place. He is excited for you and your family. He can't wait to have you guys come and be part of his church."

She persisted. "You said every church was God's church, though. How come I have to be baptized by a pastor I don't know when I could be baptized by a pastor I do know? I don't like that. You worked hard too. We are supposed to baptize me together."

I had no rebuttal to those statements. I could not argue with the theology behind them, nor did I believe any words that came out of my mouth would be helpful. So I did what ministers must do in those moments—I stalled.

"Okay. Okay, I understand what you are saying now. I am going to call your mom. She and I will think through some things and then try to figure out how this will work."

Callie smiled at my response and hugged me tight. "I'm gonna be baptized like my family!" She clapped her hands and quickly made her way over to the small gaggle of friends who were her closest companions. I knew she would have to tell them all about her excitement.

That evening, I spoke with Callie's mother. She wanted me to be the person to baptize her daughter too. She told me that her family would happily join the congregation that was willing to welcome them all with open arms, but she wanted to honor Callie's request and the relationship we had built over the past few months of theological study. Part of me was overjoyed to be given the gift of such recognition by this family, but the rest of me wondered how I was going to keep my job through the logistical nightmare that was headed my way. I did the only thing I could do: I prayed. The next day, I commenced conversations with the director of pastoral services at Hickory Ridge. My performance of any religious rite could not be on behalf of our organization because we were not a church. After a meeting with some of his colleagues and advisers, he instructed me to reach out to the pastor with whom I had been working throughout this process. He hoped the pastor would have some idea of how we might reach a resolution to this complicated situation. The pastor, a good, moderately minded Baptist, heard Callie's request and had to draw out a diagram to sort through the intermingled logistics. The family would be a member of his congregation. The family would meet with him before the baptism, and Callie would make her public profession before the community of faith she was going to join. However, I would be the minister actually performing the baptism on the day she was "dunked." He saw no problem with this arrangement because other ministers and missionaries had baptized family members who were part of his congregation before. Then it dawned on him that I was a woman. Apparently, that complicated things a bit more. The kind pastor asked me for a few minutes to make a telephone call. I was happy to extend that kindness because I was completely bound up by the stress of our situation.

I walked into the beautiful sanctuary adorned with intricate, antique woodwork, the smell of Murphy's Oil Soap indicating a fresh polish that highlighted every detail. In that quiet sanctuary, I found myself wanting to apologize for being me. If I were not a woman, this would not be a problem. If I had asked someone else to take over the faith training early on, this would not be happening. I hated that the details of my identity were complicating something that Callie had worked so hard to achieve. I even felt a twinge of anger at the God I love for creating such a messy circumstance for Callie's celebration. In the quiet of that sanctuary, I had an internal argument with the God I adore. I wanted to be a good minister.

I wanted to be the pastor Callie thought I was. I was angry because I did not believe I would ever be able to become that pastor because the fact that I am a woman would stand in the way.

In the midst of my silent argument with God, my pastor friend came sauntering into the sanctuary.

"Well, I talked to the chair of our deacons. We have a meeting tonight. Now, there has never been a lady baptize anybody in this church. It just ain't happened here before. I do think that if I explain the situation, the deacons will probably have no trouble letting you be the first. They are a good group of guys, and they will understand this to be a special situation. I don't think there will be any problem."

I smiled at his words and his intentional protection of Callie's celebration. "Thank you so much for helping me figure out a way to help her find a place to belong and be loved. She has worked so hard for this and will get so much from being part of this congregation."

I intentionally downplayed the point surrounding my part in the baptism. I did not want to press it as vital. I was going to find a way to help Callie get the baptismal celebration she had worked for and deserved. The fact that she would be welcome was enough, whether or not my participation was welcomed too. He smiled, nodded his head, and thanked me for teaching our young friend the importance of her choice to claim her faith for herself.

The next evening I received a telephone call from the pastor. After an hour-long discussion, the diaconate had decided to allow me to perform the baptism on behalf of their congregation. He offered me congratulations for being the first woman to ever "dunk a soul" in their baptistery, and he offered his apology for how difficult the process had become because of my gender. I told him that it was fine because it was not the first bump I had encountered, nor did I believe it would be the last.

The next morning, I let Callie know I would be performing her baptism and that her mom needed to call the church to schedule a Sunday that worked for their family. She was so excited that she could not wait to let her mother know. She borrowed my cell phone to call her at work and share the news. I could hear her giggles and squeals through the closed door. I wanted to join in with my own squealing. I had never performed a baptism outside of a hospital before. I had already scheduled a lesson on proper form and procedure with my pastor. There had been an opportunity to practice those details while I was in seminary, but I happened to be eight months pregnant during that time, so I had elected to wait.

This was an anxious and exciting time for me too. I was grateful to be the minister whom Callie chose to stand with her in the waters of baptism. I was working hard to put the struggles I felt in regard to the complexities of being a woman on the back shelf for now. I tried to pretend that my gender should not matter; it was not a point of importance at all. In hindsight, I probably should have addressed those struggles directly. But God found a way to help me find my truth despite my choice to ignore the significance of my female identity.

Finally, the Sunday of the baptism had come. I pressed my black clergy robe to wear into the baptistery. I was so proud of that robe; it was like the robes worn by my pastors at Lexington Avenue Baptist Church during my teenage years. It was a symbol that removed the importance of my gender identity and helped remind me that my identity in Christ was all that mattered. I found my value in knowing I was a vessel of something much bigger than myself; even if I was a cracked and crooked vessel, I was working on behalf of God. Everything was going to be all right.

I dressed in a modest, comfortably fitting black dress that communicated exceptional professionalism. The dress also made me feel pretty, something I value especially during my Sunday morning routine. I packed extra clothes too, as I did not have a pair of waders like my pastor. Honestly, I was afraid I would fall if I tried to use anything like that anyway. Instead, I packed a bathing suit and some long shorts to wear under my robe. I had called Callie the night before and reminded her that she would need extra clothes too. I had memorized the Scripture I would recite. I had gone over the process. I was ready—at least I hoped so.

I arrived at the church before Callie and her family. The pastor walked me through the logistics of getting in and out of the baptistery for the event. He explained how the service was going to flow and told me when Callie and I should begin making our way into the sanctuary from the adjoining rooms. I paid careful attention and made certain I memorized every detail so that I could relay them to Callie when she arrived. Memorization was not her strong suit, so I would have to make certain that I could repeat the instructions in a succinct, clear way more than once. After the pastor walked me through the service order, I took my extra clothes and towel into the dressing room where Callie and I would wait before the service. I placed the swimsuit and the shorts on the same hanger, facing the door. I laid one towel on the floor to absorb the water that would drip off of me, and I placed one for Callie and one for myself on a chair near the door we would walk through. I also hung my clergy robe by the door, straightening the gathered sleeves and collar over and over again. It was a really pretty, albeit simple, robe.

Callie and her family arrived a little later than expected. Her younger sisters had created some difficulty when they were asked to put on "church clothes." Callie rolled her eyes and reiterated to her mother, "I told you. God doesn't care about the dress. He cares that you show up and listen."

I laughed. This was a theological conversation she and I had had many times leading up to this celebration. She was right; Jesus wore a dress but only because nobody in his family knew how to sew pants yet. This was her logic, and, for all practical purposes, it was historically accurate. I was just happy to see that her entire family had come to be a part of her day. I pulled out the service order and went through it with my friend and her mom. I showed her the towels I had laid out and then I asked her where her change of clothing was. She looked at me, smiled a familiar, sheepish smile, and said, "Oh, I forgot that part."

I looked at her with surprise. "So what are you going to do for clothes underneath your robe?"

Her mother looked puzzled. She pointed at the black clergy robe and asked if it was for Callie. I told her I would wear the black robe and Callie would wear one of three white robes that were hanging on the other side of the room. She had a panicked look on her face now too. Callie had to have something else on under a white robe. I hadn't known ahead of time that she would need something extra. My previous church had used dark robes. What were we going to do?

"It will be all right," I assured them. "Just give me a second to think through some options. I'll be right back."

I left the dressing room and went into the bathroom. I had no ideas, no options, but I did have to pee. I thought that would at least buy me some time to find a creative solution. After releasing the anxiety that was emanating from my over-full bladder, I collected myself and went to the sink to wash my hands. I looked into the mirror and saw that my slip was still crumpled on one side. I smoothed it out and had an irritating revelation.

That morning I had put on my prettiest, most professional clergy dress with my conservative, tasteful pumps. I looked nice, but there were some bumps where I preferred to have curves. Seeing the bumps, I had elected to put on a black lace bra slip that was a ridiculous gift given to me by my husband on our second Valentine's day as husband and wife. The lingerie was surprisingly comfortable and did a great deal for my "fluffy" physique when I wore it. It was also made of a lightweight chiffon lace that dried quickly. I was faced with one of those moments when a choice becomes obvious and another voice in my head responds, "What are you thinking?!"

I smoothed my slip again, breathed deeply, and made my way back to the dressing room. I looked Callie in the eye and told her that I had brought a bathing suit for her to wear. Her mom looked at me with surprise. "I thought you were wearing the bathing suit," she said.

"I found something else I can wear under my robe. Don't worry. No one can see through a black robe anyway."

I prayed that my words were true. I could just imagine that robe floating up to reveal a black lace negligée worn by the very first female minister ever to set foot in this baptistery. The situation felt so thoroughly ridiculous that I had to laugh as we waited for the time of baptism in the service. The moment came, and together we made our way down the steps of the glass-walled pool on the side of the sanctuary. My robe did float up a bit, but I was able to push it down quickly so no one would see my pretty underwear.

As I stood in the warm waters holding my friend's hand and listening to the church's pastor offer introductions and prayer, I found myself distracted by two vivid images dancing in my thoughts. In my mind's eye, I could see my tiny, country-proper grandmother shaking her head in disapproval that I even owned a black lace slip, more disappointed that I had chosen to wear something so risqué to church, and even more disappointed that I wore it under a minister's robe during a baptism! I felt my cheeks blushing at the thoughts of her disapproval. On the other side, I could see the face of the Jesus I love laughing so hard that tears rolled down his face. The negligée was good enough for my Jesus, but it wasn't good enough for my grandmother.

I shook my head slightly to refocus on the present moment. It was an invaluable experience for me and for someone I had supported through the process of claiming her faith for herself. I found my peace when I looked into Callie's eyes; they sparkled with excitement. It turns out that I was telling the truth. Everything was fine; every part of her baptism was working out beautifully. I let myself stay in the joy of the moment. I raised my hand and asked Callie to make her declaration. Her reply is a permanent recording in my mind: "Jesus Christ is my Lord and Savior." I helped her bend down to submerge herself in the water and stand again, steadying herself on my shoulder as she did, thoroughly drenched and glowing with radiant joy.

I was overwhelmed with simultaneous humility and pride for us both. This young woman had worked diligently to claim her faith and profess it loudly in front of anyone who would listen. I, on the other hand, was ready to flee from publicly claiming my identity as a minister because I did not want to make waves or create discomfort. It was Callie who had insisted I stand up and proclaim my calling into ministry. And it was Callie's absent-minded excitement that led me to perform my ministerial duties while wearing an unmistakably feminine black lace slip underneath my robe. This ironic, humorous moment of ministry brought an important clarity to my pastoral identity: it is not possible to walk in the duties of ministry and omit the vital element of my womanhood. God called me to become a minister. The Holy Spirit reiterated the ceaseless, booming whisper that helped me choose my vocational path. A sister in Christ who had been considered "less than" many of those around her insisted I stop being ashamed of who I was made to become. I had been her advocate and she had been mine. As I helped her claim her identity as a member of the Body of Christ, we both found our separate truths, recognizing the kinship of the souls that joined us together in unexpected, stunning grace.

Questions for the Soul

1. Can you embrace the fullness of your identity, or do you hide parts of yourself in fear?

2. What does professing your faith mean to you? Why?

3. What has God given you to help you be brave?

Chapter 4

JIM'S REVELATION

I came to Hickory Ridge through an interwoven happenstance at the end of my chaplain residency at Baptist Health Louisville. I was thirty years old and had completed my Master of Divinity at Baptist Seminary of Kentucky. I had been an outstanding student throughout my graduate studies, and I had earned nods from many professional organizations. I sought titles and credentials to validate a calling that felt so paradoxical to the understanding I had for myself as a clumsy, confounding, and altogether deficient human being. I thought credentials would help me feel more worthy of serving as an ambassador for the God I dearly loved, so I collected as many as I possibly could along my professional path.

When the time came to move into my first independent office, I was exceedingly thrilled at the validation of my importance alongside a professional team of caregivers. I had *arrived*. Within my first week at work, I submitted a request to maintenance to hang my many diplomas, certifications, and credentials on my office wall. There were plenty of them too, an obnoxious collection for certain. I came in the afternoon after our interdisciplinary meeting and almost squealed with delight as I saw them hanging on the wall behind my desk. They filled nearly the entire wall, and I was so proud. I propped my door open to "get more air," but I was also aware that I would be able to show off my wall of hubris to everyone passing by. I had barely gotten the doorstop in place when I heard the familiar squeak of an electric wheelchair pausing in front of the doorway. I looked up and saw my friend Jim. He had lived at Hickory Ridge since the beginning of its existence. Jim was a cantankerous, quirky, and funny man who loved to push people's buttons. I was happy to see him, especially since he was staring at the freshly adorned wall that demonstrated my incredible skills in the field of ministry. He asked, "Pastor Kate, what is all that stuff you got up on your wall there?"

I felt happy to have the chance to explain the "self-shrine" to him. "That's my most important stuff, Jim. I spent a lot of time and money to get all that stuff there. I worked hard for it."

"Worked hard for it, huh?" He looked confused as he listened.

"I did. That's expensive stuff on that wall." I was trying to help him understand the value of my beautiful frames of validation.

He still looked confused as he turned his gaze from the wall and then back toward me. He said, "Well, that's a damn shame." He gave me a crooked grin and waited for my eyes to meet his. "They ain't even pretty, just a bunch of words on paper." After he had dropped his grounding bomb, he pushed the joystick on his wheelchair and rolled on down the hallway, shaking his head while laughing.

With that one commentary, Jim planted the seed for the life lesson that my congregation at Hickory Ridge would teach me over and over again through the years: authority and validation are not things you can earn through the course of academia or pay to maintain with a credentialing entity. Authority in caring relationships is based on caring and not much else, particularly in the culture of this blessed place. The people I support don't care much about how many degrees I have on the wall; they would rather see drawings they made for me or pictures of us together enjoying life. I tell people that I write and teach and speak at many different venues for a lot of reasons, but mostly because I am indebted to the people who call me their pastor. I have a lot of training, but I did not really understand the love of God until I was loved by these people and given the blessing of loving them in return. This book is my way of offering some of the wisdom they have shared with this world that so desperately needs to hear their unique truth.

The foundations of Relational Spirituality are found in the reciprocal give and take of human relationships. An endless humility is required for weaving authentic, transformational relationships. We are shaped by the interactions we have with those around us. We are also shaped by the ways our mind and history perceive our experience, things we may never share with the world outside of our own thoughts. The people we meet help define our identity in many ways. We seek our reflection in the eyes of those we encounter. Daniel Siegel's work on mindfulness and the response of mirror neurons throughout human interactions demonstrates a scientific foundation for this desperate need. Our very biology is wired to intermingle our identity with that of those we meet. It is not a flaw in our character to seek definition within the community that upholds us; it is an error to seek this external definition apart from the rest of our identity. The mind, body, heart, and soul all seek a different rendering of our "self." It is not surprising that the complexity of this self-identification sometimes gets stalled in the various stages of our development. We can remain in places of fear, refusing to take responsibility for the lives we choose to lead. We can stay where people we love have formed an emotional fencing to keep us safe, or we can force a façade of "sameness" in our everyday lives. And we sometimes allow these things because it is easier to let others say who we are than it is to fight past all of the ugliness lurking in the blind spots of our self-awareness. We hide in plain sight, neglecting the fullness of our place in the world and settling for living in the light of only our material contribution to the world.

Living only for tangible productivity can become terribly lonely when age and transition remove our ability to contribute. When we can't "do" anything anymore, are we still ourselves? How will we know?

I don't believe Jim's question was intended to be a kick in the gut, but he may have been intentionally cantankerous. That playful and commanding spirit was, after all, one of the funniest and most endearing parts of his personality. He was a frail old man in some ways, but he was also a giant in the small community of people working and living at Hickory Ridge. He was known for his flirtatious ways and the manipulative tactics he used to spend time with people throughout the Hickory Ridge family. He was a legend of sorts, and he knew it.

Jim was not being hostile in his statement, but he was being clear. After he called my credentials "a damn shame," he cocked his mouth in a sideways grin and waited for me to truly see him. I looked into his big brown eyes and was utterly ticked off. Who did he think he was?

Jim didn't think he was anything. Jim knew he was the authority in the teaching friendship we would nurture over the next six years of our lives. He would constantly bicker with me and other members of his support team to make sure we knew he would choose his path, his goals, and his journey. He had one remarkable gift: he knew how to irritate everyone he loved, and he knew how to make them love him despite the frustration. He was tender. He was wise. He truly loved people he took on as a part of himself.

I was blessed to hold his hand through the loss of many friends. I stood beside him as he cradled and kissed the face of the woman he had loved for decades right after her death. In all of our years together, Jim spoke one great kindness to me. It was a blessing out of nowhere that changed how I thought about myself forever. He looked me in the eye, offered his crooked grin, and said, "Pastor Kate, I love you for no reason at all. I love you just cuz you is."

Years after he passed on to the next life that was his reward, I still cling to that beautiful blessing on days when I feel lost. Jim's love was akin to that of our Almighty Abba, the great Father who blesses our every breath simply because we breathe. When my strength is tapped out and my sense of productivity is confounded by all that I cannot achieve, I remember that I am loved because I am, and I let myself be overwhelmed by the gratitude of that truth.

When I have worked past my own strength and I cannot find the root of my identity, I step into the wisdom Jim left me. I am the authority of my identity; pieces of paper on a wall mean very little. I choose how I respond. I choose what I value most. I choose how I live out the giftedness that God has invested in me. Jim taught me to claim the freedom I have as a human being and a child of God. I honor my love for him and his love for me by holding on to that irrefutable truth when I am tempted to bury myself under the yoke of over-functioning and to grasp for brass rings that I may never reach. I choose my freedom.

Questions for the Soul

1. Who are you?

2. How do you know?

3. What will you do with that awareness?

Chapter 5

ROSIE'S WISDOM

Rosie was a sweet, feisty little Irish woman whose eyes shone with a love of life. When I met her, she was more than fifty years old and used a wheelchair. She had significant health problems aside from the Down syndrome that brought her to Hickory Ridge. She had lived among that community for more than thirty years and made certain that her expertise and authority were noted. Despite her prolonged tenure as a queen among us, she always offered her correction, displeasure, and constructive criticism with grace and Southern charm. Rosie seldom lost her temper, but when she did it was generally in interactions with her best friend, Carry. Though Carry lacked Rosie's genteel manner, the two women had been best friends since they became roommates in the earliest days of Hickory Ridge. Carry was prone to jokes with off-color language and innuendo and loved to watch Rosie cover her eyes from embarrassment after the punch line. The two ladies would fight and giggle with the same fire that wove together the intricate nature of their deep love for one another. When one was sick, the other would make certain to send me or Pastor Mark to check on her friend and pray with her. When one was offended, the other would take up arms, wheeling herself to the perpetrator and verbally accosting that person for hurting her best friend. Though they bickered, they were bound by heart and soul.

The day Carry died, I was present when Rosie learned of her passing. She seemed to lose her breath for a moment and then wept on the shoulder of a staff member and friend who had loved her for decades. She wept for her loss and wept for the hurt of us all. I watched from a distance, not wanting to intrude on her pain; the kind of love those two women shared had earned time and space for sorrow. I remember barely holding myself together as she cried. I watched for a while and then made my way to the chapel to sit in the dark and quiet and mourn. Being present for the heartache of those we love requires that we be present and aware of our own heartache, separating the two before we fulfill our function as a spiritual guide through the journey of loss. After a few minutes of sorrow and powerlessness, I made my way to the staff restroom, splashed water on my face, and tried to gather myself before heading back out to check on Rosie.

As I walked toward the wing of our building that Rosie called home, I saw her seated beside the nurse's desk at the front of the living room. She was holding hands with the suite nurse, Dorothy, who had been with her throughout most of her time at Hickory Ridge. The two of them were talking and laughing as they told stories. I was struck by their laughter.

I wondered how Rosie had regrouped so quickly. I walked up to the women and asked if I could pull up a chair.

"Well, sure you can. Sit here," Rosie answered with her usual, sweet Southern drawl. She pointed to the space next to her wheelchair. The nurse, who needed to give other residents their medications, rose to leave. She smiled at me, winked, and nodded before she walked away. I knew this nurse. She loved Rosie and Carry fiercely. Her reassuring wink and nod said to me, "You can do this, and God will help you do it well."

I pulled my chair next to Rosie, facing her. This is the best position for speaking closely with—and hugging—someone in a wheelchair: eye to eye, never looking down on them. I smiled at Rosie and she opened our conversation with, "Good morning, beautiful."

Rosie's affirmations had always reminded me of my grandmother, and this welcome brought her to mind just like so many others before it. I took note and began the conversation from my side. "Well, thank you, Rosie. I wanted to come check on you. How are you doing?"

"I'm all right. I'm doing just okay."

"Are you? I came to check on you because I know how much you loved your Carry and how hard it is to lose somebody you love like that." My concern must have been present in my furrowed brow because she gave me a nod and her hospitable, chubby-faced grin.

"Yeah. It is hard. I mean it *is* hard, but I'm okay. It'll be okay. I get to go next."

My breath caught and I found my grounding again. "What do you mean, you 'get to go next'?" I was praying she hadn't gotten confused and thought that Carry had gone to another place or activity. Suicidal commentary from Rosie was not something I was prepared to address. Though ministers are not supposed to have favorite clients or patients, Rosie had easily become very special to me. Her grace and stature, her bright blue eyes, and her sassy wit reminded me so much of my grandmother that I could not help some intermingling within myself of the love I held for both women.

"I mean I'll be all right until it's time for me to go too. I'm okay." She nodded again and patted my forearm.

"Well, good, I'm glad you are okay. I was worried about you. It's awful sad losing somebody you loved for so long."

"Oh, I am sad. I'm very sad. But it *has* to be okay." Rosie repeated herself, looking squarely into my eyes. She wanted me to know she had not lost her sadness or the absence of her friend. She also wanted to teach me something of her faith and wisdom. I saw her intense gaze and knew she intended to meet me in this moment, soul to soul, so that I could glimpse some of the precious wisdom she had gained through her life's journey.

"You don't *have* to be okay. Who says you *have* to be okay?" I asked.

People frequently try to stifle tears in the midst of loss so as to avoid the uncomfortable process of grief. I do my best to dissuade this habitual response from many staff, but the care that is offered from our direct staff is interwoven with a great deal of emotional investment. Most of the time this care is a gift, but in some cases it creates a bit of harm. People are frequently inclined to silence or redirect suffering when there is no immediate fix. In rural cultures, this is part of survival and coping in a world that has deep loss and struggle at its foundation. This is the culture of most direct support professionals at Hickory Ridge, and it happens to be my own. In this culture, we learn to live on, to keep working, to tend the crops despite major losses. We learn to do this so that our families and our farms endure, so that a harvest will sustain us once the immediate ache has dulled.

"Ooh honey, you are young." Rosie smiled and laughed, shaking her head. "I cry sometimes. I cry when things are really sad because some things in this world are really sad. I cry and then I cry some more. But then I have to stop crying because some things just 'are,' and God says that has to be okay, at least for now."

She looked into my eyes with a tender clarity that was unique to her pale, freckled Irish beauty. I clenched my jaw to hold back my tears. I was struck by the sincere clarity of her faith; it was so beautiful that it astounded me. Was this an embodiment of faith I could ever understand? Would I ever be strong enough to submit to the world's brokenness in order to see the big picture even in my heartache?

"That sounds awful wise, Miss Rosie." I smiled and took her hand.

"Well, you know, I've been around a long time." She laughed again and squeezed my hand in her tiny, pale ones.

"You have, and I hope you'll be around even longer."

She smiled and slightly shook her head again. "No, I'll get to see my Carry again soon. It'll be my turn next." She let go of my hand and patted the top of it as she spoke.

I was struck by her comments, both by her beautiful surrender to the heartbreak of this world and also by her fearless understanding of her own death.

In the days that followed, Rosie continued to live her life, laughing and joking, nurturing, bickering, and cherishing every moment. She did mourn her friend, weeping as she shared stories in preparation for the funeral mass. She wept and laid her hand on the casket that day too. Then, a few weeks after Carry's death, Rosie fell ill. After two weeks of sitting with Rosie and her family at her bedside, I called in the priest who would offer her final anointing. Though she had to be in some pain, she still smiled and held his hand as he offered the sacrament for her impending death. She was mostly worried about her family and friends. I promised her I would hug them and stay with them during their sadness.

Rosie died six weeks after her best friend Carry. Throughout her time in the hospital prior to her end, she did not flinch. She reassured staff, her family, and even her young nurse. She told us she was going to be just fine, that she could see her mother and Carry and the most beautiful angel. These types of hallucinations are not uncommon during the dying process, but I had no doubt that Rosie actually saw each of these images. She was a four-foot, eight-inch spiritual giant who was wrapped in the warmth of a steadfast faith up to her very last breath. Years since her passing, Rosie's grace in life and death still stands out as one of the most precious experiences of unbridled faith that I have ever known.

Rosie's love for Carry was bigger than I understood. She loved Carry enough to bicker with her, to push her, to compete with her, to offer kindness, and to offer laughter whenever it was necessary. They had a common struggle in their disabilities but also a common resilience in their tenacious life full of passion and meaning. Rosie surrendered to the "bigger picture" in the loss of her beloved best friend. She ached for her loss but made way for Carry's freedom in her grief too. Carry wasn't fighting illnesses and limitations anymore, not in Rosie's dreams. Carry didn't need her wheelchair anymore, like the days when they were younger; she was surrounded by the beloved family that she cherished. She was a part of something bigger than memory and loss can encompass. Rosie did not crave death, but she did not fear it either. She did not fear loss. She did not rage against the powerlessness of her situation. Instead, she took it into herself as a regular part of the human condition.

I have never been a woman who would readily surrender to anyone or anything. I fight all the time, even when there is no real reason to fight! Sometimes I fight in preparation for a fight that may or may not take place. Miss Rosie taught me that one way of "fighting" is to surrender. This type of fight is above and against ourselves. We battle the pride and anxiety within ourselves. Relinquishing the façade of control offers an enlightened sense of freedom in the life of the faithful. It feels like a sophomoric response in the beginning, but after practice, there is a solid certainty that I do not have to know the answers. I do not have to repair the most painful corners of human experience. There is a time to surrender and lift up prayers to the God I say I love more than all else. There is a time to stop fighting against powerlessness and recognize the precious innocence that accompanies those moments. They are a cornerstone of the human experience. We were intended to know that struggle; it is the struggle of the loving Christ atop Golgotha's hill when the pain of this life overwhelms and all worldly hope is lost.

Questions for the Soul

1. What role does fear play in our response to grief? Why?

2. What stands between us and "surrender" in the face of this world's powerless moments?

3. How did Rosie's view of the "bigger picture" influence her understanding of death?

4. What might we take away from that perception for our own journey?

Chapter 6

WHO BLESSES WHOM

Isaac was a unique, funny, lovable guy, albeit frustrating at times. He had a way of wiggling his endearing, stubborn soul into your heart like I imagine a little brother would. He was a man of few words, but he could always communicate what he wanted in any given moment. He would stare at me with his glass-blue eyes and baby face and wrap my heart around his arthritic fingers in a moment. Isaac had lived at Hickory Ridge for all of his adult life, well over thirty years. He had his favorite staff people, his mother, his friends in the community, and those who had been his room-mates throughout his life in our facility. He was a happy man, but he did struggle. His health was fragile. He was born with Down syndrome, a heart condition, and significant kidney troubles and had developed severe arthritis as he aged. I was not only privileged to know him throughout the last few years of his life but also to become a pastor to him.

Isaac was fond of teasing and irritating people. It seemed he was testing them to measure how invested they were in knowing and loving him. When he met me, he found that I had a great desire to know him well. For the first couple of years I attempted to know and support him, he would close his eyes every time I came to speak to him. As I lingered in front of him, trying to speak to a man with his eyes closed, he would cover his ears and begin yelling. I recognized this passive aggressive move; it had been a favorite of my little sister while we were growing up. She would usually break out her "can't hear you, can't see you" move when I was trying to convince her to take a bath at night. It frustrated me then too, but I did develop some strategies to overcome my invisibility in that relationship. My baby sister taught me to wait in the midst of those irregular arguments. All she needed was to know that she was calling the shots, making her own choices. I gathered that my friend Isaac was trying to secure a similar power. With this awareness, I learned to drop my agenda for acceptance and pay attention to who Isaac was. He was flirtatious, playful, and loyal to those he allowed into his heart. My bubbly, overly anxious, appeasing self was not the authentic me, and he knew that. He demanded that I meet him as I was. And so I did. I would sit alongside him, quietly watching him engage those he held dear. I practiced this every week for a few months until one day he stopped ignoring me. It was nearing the end of the class session he and I were attending. I was there observing him and a new individual so that I could gain insight into their way of interacting with people and communicating. I had gathered up my notes and was waiting for the class members to begin their exit toward lunch in the dining room. As I sat, I heard Isaac's familiar beckoning holler. I looked in his direction and saw him pointing at me as he bellowed. I smiled and he laughed at my expression. He then motioned me to come over.

I had come to know the man well enough that I was expecting him to point to the handles on his wheelchair as a way of requesting that I help him get to the dining room before all the good desserts were chosen. I stood up, shook my head, and made my way toward him. If nothing else, I appreciated the predictability of our interactions now. However, my prediction was not on target this time. When I reached his side, I laid my notebooks and pencils on the table beside him. "Do I need to help you get the goods in the dining room, sir?" I smiled down at his bright face.

He looked at me, grinning so wide that his brilliant blue eyes were nearly closed by the lift of his cheeks. Again he raised his hand and called me closer to him with his waving index finger. I leaned down, complying with his request. As I got closer, he pushed himself up taller in his wheelchair and planted a joyful, wet kiss on my cheek. I felt myself flinch in surprise. I just looked at him with my eyes wide open. He then patted my hand and relaxed back down into his chair again.

I was confounded. What was different about today? How had I met his level of acceptability differently today than any other day? I think that he finally recognized my investment and decided that, perhaps, I needed a little investment from him too. I wasn't sure where the change in direction originated, but I was exuberant with what felt like a conquest of his stubborn will. I did not know then, but I do know now, that the conquest was never mine and had little to do with his acceptance of me. The next few days came and went, and I was offered the same display of affection during my time with Isaac. Even funnier than his simple display of care was his response to the smile it always brought to my face. He would watch and wait for me to smile in response to his offering of care. After I did, he would grin and relax back down into his chair. He had done his good deed for the day. He had worked to repair what was slowly mending within my spirit. We continued this relational dance of give and take in the vernacular of acceptance and affirmation until one Friday when he was missing from class. In his place, I was met by his staff member, who was assisting another individual in her transition from one place to the next. I asked her where Isaac was, and she told me that he had been taken to the hospital early that morning because he was unresponsive when she attempted to wake him. I felt my heart skip a beat and sink. I closed my eyes, took a deep breath, and remembered my job in this place. I was a minister, a chaplain, a supportive presence. In my moment of dread, I could not address my own anxiety yet. At least, I could not address it with complete transparency. I asked her if a staff person had gone to the hospital with him. She responded that someone had gone, but the person was supposed to go off shift an hour ago. She wasn't sure if anyone was there with him now.

"I can go check to see if they need somebody to wait with him," I said. "I'm sure that will make things easier for the supervisors, anyway. I'll let you know how he's doing when I get back."

I saw her relief. I also felt the load lightened from my shoulders when I found a way to be near someone I loved as he was struggling. Cantankerous and finicky as he was, that man had become my friend and I loved him.

I hurried to the local hospital, anxious about what I would see when I was able to track him down. I have been a chaplain, and I understand that death is part of life. Death is not necessarily something to be feared by those who are nearing their end. Death seems most terrifying to those who are left behind. I was not ready to be left behind by Isaac, but I would never be the authority who could choose if that would be the outcome for anyone I loved.

I walked into his room and saw him sitting upright, legs wadded up in his normal pretzel twist position. He did look pail and tired, but he was certainly not gone. I caught the tears in my eyes as he turned my way and motioned for me to come closer to his hospital bed. I mirrored his smile and made my way over to him. He took my hand and pulled me into a big hug. I was happily surprised to be greeted with such excitement. I looked around and saw that no staff was in the room with him, but someone had been there. His backpack was sitting close by with a note pinned to the top. The staff person had written instructions for Isaac's care. It was a short list detailing how to understand which gestures meant yes, which meant no, and how to look at his forehead to see if he were in pain. The closing line had the phone number of Hickory Ridge's Health Services Coordinator and a final "Please tell him we all love him and someone is on their way to be with him."

There was a round, bubble heart drawn at the end of the sentence. I assumed the staff person I had met in the classroom earlier had already let her know I was on my way so she could leave to be with her children. I am still amazed at how a force of so many diverse and different staff members can be so closely knit together by their devotion to the people we support. It is a miraculous side effect of the beauty inside the walls of our little universe. I'm forever grateful for the chance to be a part of this community, loved and trusted because time and tenacity have proven I am worthy.

I straightened the room a bit, singing "Jeremiah Was a Bullfrog" as I did. It is not the holiest of ballads, but it was one that Isaac loved. He especially liked to hear me sing it. I sang and gathered all of his things together. I moved the pinned note to a more prominent place, attached to the bottom of his vitals monitor. It would be hard to overlook there. Once I finished, I sat next to my friend, turning my chair to face him easily. I leaned forward, offered my smile, and asked, "Are you hangin' in there, my brother?"

He looked at me, nodded, and uttered an easy, "Yeah."

"Are you feeling a mite better now? You had us worried this morning."

He smiled, nodded again, and repeated, "Yeah."

"Is there anything I can do for you while I'm here? I can't do a whole lot, but I'll offer whatever I can."

He smiled, and then he did something I had never seen him do before. He put his hands together, fingers stretched out long and touching each other to form the quintessential praying hands that Christians see throughout worship publications in all corners of our tradition.

I looked at him with confusion. "You want me to pray?"

I must have had a terrible expression of puzzlement on my face because he threw his head back and let out a loud belly laugh. Then he looked back at me, nodded, and said, "Yeah." He pointed to his forehead as he answered.

I knew he had spent his early years as a member of the Catholic church, but I also knew he had not practiced his faith with a priest for years because he preferred to spend the time allotted for Catholic services in our community visiting with friends or his mother.

I struggled with how to uphold his faith and still offer him something. "I'm not Catholic, nor a priest or anything else like that. I can only offer you a Baptist prayer for right now and a promise to find a priest or Eucharistic minister to come give you what I can't. Will that do for right now?"

He smiled again, patting my hand as he nodded. He repositioned himself in his bed, straightening his posture and leaning his head toward me. To see his face with such an invitation to a practice of faith overwhelmed me. I was certainly going to give him some semblance of what he needed until I could find a proper clergyperson for him.

He held his straight posture, closed his eyes, and pointed to his forehead. I placed my hand on his cheek and he opened his eyes to see me again.

"I will do my best. You tell me if I need to fix anything, okay?"

"Yeah."

I waited for his eyes to meet mine again before I made the symbol of a cross in the center of his forehead, as even we Baptists do during celebrations of Holy Week. I spoke the words of genuine prayer from the depths of my being. "God bless your beautiful soul. In the name of the Father, the Son, and the Holy Spirit. Amen."

His grin grew even bigger as I finished.

"Did I get it right?" I asked him to make certain I had not offended with my unrefined attempt to bless a soul I loved so dearly.

In his way, he smiled, nodded, and said, "Yeah." Then he patted me on top of my head like a child who had reached her goal and pleased the teacher. In that moment, I felt the most conflicting jumble of humility and empowerment that I had known in my recent practice of ministry. I watched Isaac settle back into his bed and fall into a restful sleep, and I was grateful to have had the time with him but even more grateful to have been able to engage in that sacred moment. I was not certain how valuable faith practice was to Isaac because he had never made it a priority in the activities and schedules of his daily life. I had assumed I was just a friendly, persistent, caring presence to him without any attachment of religiosity. How mistaken I had been. He asked for a blessing that I felt unprepared to give, he received my clumsy attempt, and he settled into a peaceful rest. In that brief interaction with my dear friend, I learned how to be his pastor. I was ordained by a tangential invitation into a holy moment. Isaac knew who I was to him; I just didn't understand what he expected from me. The humbling part of the process was the invitation and the instruction that walked me into that ordination.

I had extended a blessing that day, and I did not even have the resources within myself to offer it. I was only able to bless and be blessed in return, with the guidance of the man who chose to commune with me as we, together, engaged in a sacred moment of submission to our faith. I surrendered to the minister I am called to be. I chose to provide the best support I could in that instance, and in doing so I chose to continue walking an uncertain path in which those I support actually help me to define my offerings of care. In his instruction to me and in the invitation to pray, Isaac relinquished the distance between us, finding comfort in the trusting prayer offered by a minister who loved him. We each found our peace in the midst of a clumsy interaction, heartfelt friendship, and a simple prayer that reminded us to trust in the faith that sustained us both.

Questions for the Soul

1. How do you engage what is sacred in your faith?

2. Whom do you trust to journey to the sacred with you?

3. How was that relationship formed?

Chapter 7

ALBERT'S SANCTUARY

Albert was a tiny man, not quite five feet tall, and he did not speak. He lived out his life with the weight of severe sensory defenses, so sound and light and commotion were painful for him. Holiday parties would result in what appeared to be bouts of terror. Albert had been placed in an institution when he was very young, in accordance with the recommendations of his family doctor. His parents were told that this would be the best course of action for him, and they trusted that the professionals advising them were right. Albert spent decades being shuffled between facilities that were underfunded, overcrowded, and not sensitive to his gentle nature. The notations of his life described a couple of occurrences of severe, almost deadly abuse that he endured during one of the transitions of his early life. When I saw him for the first time, I recognized his fear. His anxious brown eyes silently called out to the fear that lived within the shadows of my memory too. It is something people who have survived ugliness learn to recognize upon meeting others like them. Our scars were not the same, but we could certainly relate to one another.

I was told that Albert was very skittish and only took to a few people in his world. As I attempted to get to know him, I discovered that these descriptions were a bit generous in terms of the people he held dear. Over the course of observing him, I saw him investing trust in only a handful of people. He normally shied away from strangers and paced the long hallways that connected suites to one another. I watched him pace and pace and pace, and I wondered if he ever stopped. The staff member he trusted most told me he did stop, but it was usually during mealtime and right before bed. As I watched him pace, I wondered how I might engage him in relationship without intruding on the safety of his control and without interfering with the pacing that seemed to provide an outlet for his fear.

First, I tried to walk alongside him, he didn't welcome the company. He looked startled as I began walking his usual path with three feet separating us along the course. He then retreated to his bedroom and closed the door. This would not be the way that I formed a relationship with Albert. He would choose to become a friend or he would not. My preference could not be the deciding factor.

I mean no insult to a man whose spirit is more beautiful that most I have known in my life, but surrendering to the choice of Albert reminded me of my early years on our family farm. When my father would buy a skittish animal at the stockyards, a cow or sheep or horse, I sometimes got to be the first in the family to meet it. My father taught me that an animal that had been hurt would be afraid to trust anyone because once a human being became a threat, all human beings became a threat. He taught me that helping an animal learn to trust again meant surrendering all of the control in the relationship to that animal, at least until a foundation of trust was laid. This process took a lot of time! My father taught me that animals interpret direct eye contact as confrontation and standing tall as a sign of power to dominate. He told me that most people interpret things that way too, whether they realize it or not. He told me animals and people are a lot alike at their core. I respect my father's wisdom in this because I have read many studies linking the nonverbal communications of the reptilian brain to that of animal instinct.

With my father's teaching in mind, I decided to offer an invitation to Albert that was like the invitations I had extended to animals as a child. I cleared an afternoon on my schedule and waited until I knew he would be pacing. I did not want to interrupt his peace, but I wanted him to know that I was around if he needed me and that I was not going to take anything from him that he did not choose to give. So I sat on the floor near the end of his path. I chose the spot for sitting because it was quiet and out of the way of everyone else. I just sat there, shifting from my knees to my bottom as time passed. I folded my hands and quieted my mind as best I could, and I waited. At the beginning of my time there, he would walk by quickly, as though he was trying to pass by without being seen. After an hour, he began slowing down as he passed me, looking in my direction. I said nothing but gently smiled when his eyes met mine. I was surprised that he did not look away; the animals I had known as a child always looked away at first. Finally, he stopped pacing when he came to my position in the hallway. He stood for a bit, and then he sat on the floor right in front of me, his eyes staring into mine without a twinge of fear. I smiled and slowly offered my hand, palm up, prepared to receive anything he would like to offer.

"Hi," I said. "I am Pastor Kate, Pastor Mark's helper. I'm pleased to finally meet you, sir."

He looked at me and placed his palm on mine without breaking eye contact. As the warmth of his hand met the warmth of mine, he smiled, let out a tiny giggle, and then quickly pulled his hand back. He stood again and resumed pacing. After our proper introduction, he gave me a tiny half grin the next time he passed me in the hallway. I sat on the cold linoleum floor for three hours that day, but that half grin was worth every ache in my back and behind. I was grateful to have won a small victory with this man, but I was also happy to discern so much about his personality. I had submitted all the power in our relationship to him, and he liked it, as demonstrated by his smile and the three hours I spent sitting on the floor. This man was smart and funny; I could tell from the way he taunted me upon our meeting. He was going to meet me, but he was only going to offer what he wanted to offer, no more or less in consideration of me. I admired his spirit.

In working with Albert, I sought a way to give him the control he needed and invite him into relationship. I began visiting him daily, making certain that I became a familiar, trustworthy part of his community. Then we progressed in our friendship, and he let me pace with him up and down the hallways; some days he even held my hand. After a month passed, I found myself feeling particularly confident and motivated to move forward. Albert and I were going to go on a walk around the local park. It was autumn in our rural community, so the scenery was breathtaking. I doubted that Albert had been given the opportunity to enjoy scenic views during his time in other facilities. Generally speaking, it is difficult for facilities to find the staffing or setting to offer this kind of opportunity. So I asked him, as we paced, "Would you want to go for a walk with me around the park?"

Albert stopped dead in his tracks, looked me in the eyes, let loose of my hand, and walked into his bedroom. I assumed that I had made him angry or frightened him with the invitation, but then his bedroom door opened. He passed through the doorway, putting on his coat and handing me his hat. Joy overwhelmed me. I was going to get to walk alongside my friend as our relationship grew into a bigger world. He had walked with others, but he had never taken this walk with me. I wondered why he was so excited to go; the revelation along our stroll in the park would be greater than most I had known during my tenure as a minister.

Albert repositioned his hat after I helped him place it on his head. After his view was unobstructed and the tops of his ears were warm, he zipped his coat and we began our walk. As we stepped onto the paved path that circled the park, he placed his hand in mine, weaving our fingers into a comfortable pattern. Then we silently walked. I did not know that the loop around this park was over a mile long and had more inclines than I remember seeing before. We came to the final hill along the path, and Albert stopped walking. I saw him lift his big brown eyes toward the horizon across from the hill where we stood. He squeezed his fingers tightly in the braid of our hands. I turned to follow his gaze and saw the horizon painted with brilliant red and orange and gold. It was still early in the day, so the glisten of dew sparkled with the motion of the trees. A small, gentle breeze blew directly into our faces. I looked at Albert and saw the biggest, brightest, most beautiful smile I had ever witnessed. My eyes filled with tears of gratitude. I loved this tiny, stubborn man, and I loved to see his dimples, but those were not the sentiments that brought about such an overwhelming emotion. For the first time in my pastoral career, I understood the breadth of worship's definition.

Albert had never participated in a formalized faith tradition. He had never had experiences with congregational worship because of his anxiety and sensory defenses. But Albert certainly knew what was sacred to him. To Albert, trust was sacred, true friendship was sacred, and the peace that filled our time atop that hill was sacred. Albert had welcomed me into his sanctuary and taught me the worship of his soul. Thank God I was smart enough to pay attention and let him. I still cherish the wisdom my friend gave me on that autumn morning and the gift of being present to opportunities for the worship of an Almighty God that could meet me, or anyone else, in any circumstance. That day, I learned that my pastoral training had given me expertise in a lot of things, but it had not offered me a concrete understanding of when, where, and how the holy would show up for the soul of someone I was supporting. I believe the humility of that lesson taught me more than cultural sensitivity; it taught me that the perfectionist spirit that I tried to appease in my work of ministry would have to die. I am not the person who can define sanctity experienced by someone else, but sometimes I do get to be present when we meet holy moments along the way. For the privilege of being present to that revelation, I will forever be grateful.

Questions for the Soul

1. What is sacred in your life, and how did it become that for you?

2. Who shares your most sacred moments with you?

3. How did the first invitation to share the sacred take place?

Epilogue

I hope that the concepts of integration and growth are evident in the stories I have shared. I hope they speak to the reciprocal nature of spiritual revelation. The Holy Spirit does not move in one direction at a time because we say so. The Holy Spirit moves through and toward each soul in the context of relationships, so the revelation is available to each member who participates in relational encounters. As we make our way through this life, I hope we make time to pause and recognize the Divine Investment of the people who cross our path. Do I know the name of the person who works the register at my grocery? Do I remember the eye color of the person who is rushing, feverishly, to bring me my dinner while dining out? Have I considered the wisdom that can come from a person living with significant disabilities? Have I looked past our difference deeply enough to appreciate our similarity? Have I learned the story of the colleague who drives me crazy during the meetings that fill my afternoons? These are the questions I present to myself at the end of each day. I repent for the opportunities i missed and the souls I glossed over in my hurry or focus on "doing" life over living it. I am thankful for the grace that offers me an opportunity to wake up and try again the next day.

The work of Relational Spirituality is the same as the work of being attuned to the sanctity of the lives we encounter every day. We choose how we will prioritize our focus and energy. We choose how we will acknowledge the people who cross our paths. In the field of spiritual support, there is room to ignore the possibility of revelation during an encounter with another soul. I am grateful to be called into this line of work. When I was younger, I never imagined being part of something so profoundly beautiful. I wanted to become an exceptional person, noted for my fame and place in society. As I grew up, I discovered that I was not made to become an exceptional person; I was made to teach through the lens of finding the exceptional spirit held within every person. Through moments of birth and death and everything in between, I find a way to see a picture that is so much bigger than any given moment or any single person's contribution. This discovery involves both great responsibility and great freedom. I am grateful to be a part of such a complex and intricate existence, and I am even more grateful to have relationships that help me see the sanctity of moments as they occur.

APPENDIX

Spiritual Life Assessment

This assessment is a presentation of information gathered from a person's records. It is gathered to create a full-context understanding of personhood. It also contains information gathered from family and staff interviews. Any statements of clinical or medical information are notes of data from professionals trained within the appropriate field of care, not assessment by Pastoral Services. All recommendations are rooted in the practice of individualized spiritual nurture for the well-being of God's children with the consideration of their unique identity.

Resident Identification

Name, Date of Birth
Gender, Eye Color
This section facilitates the staff process of "centering" on the individual being assessed.

Diagnoses Pertinent to Environmental and Social Factors

This section contains information that affects how staff communicates with and walks alongside the person they are supporting. Seizure disorders, diabetes, significant allergies, cardiac and/or pulmonary conditions are also in this section as valuable information for staff supporting individuals outside of Hickory Ridge.

This section is intended to help staff be aware of needs present in their interactions with the person they are supporting. Spiritual Life staff also use this information in the preparation for day trips or in planning community congregational worship.

Interpersonal Considerations

This section includes interpersonal interaction notes (nonverbal expressions of anxiety, discomfort, and/or happiness), communication styles with specific details (volume, timbre, and pitch of speech preferred), and environmental considerations for this person (e.g., aversion to crowds, fear of severe weather, etc.).

This section is intended to be a "translation key" for staff engaging this person in all forms of communication and relationship.

Social/Faith History

This section includes details of birth, early life, milestones, and diagnostic history if it is pertinent to the developmental process of the person being assessed. For example, individuals diagnosed with degenerative disease processes require continual grief support surrounding the independent functions they have lost. Education history, faith/religious details, and meaningful relationships for this individual help to provide distinct cultural awareness for the staff. This section may also include soothing methods that are effective for this person.

*All of this information is most effective when composed in a succinct biographical narrative format. Neurological synthesis of the information presented as narrative includes more emotional engagement by the reader and creates an effective invitation for staff into relationship.

Suggested Special Services/Activities

This section contains notes regarding familiar relationships and the routines associated for the individual described. It is a valuable tool for all members of the support team. Favorite pastimes, hobbies, activities, places, and artistic expressions are included for use by the care team.

Recommendations for Spiritual Support

This section contains recommendations specific to the Pastoral Services Department. Recommendations are given for invitation to participate in worship services, as chosen, at Hickory Ridge or in an appropriate community congregation. Congregations are determined by applying the individual's faith history, sensory needs, and cultural preference. We also recommend some type of interaction with Pastoral Services staff that facilitates familiarity and comfort (prayer, walking, laughing, coloring, music making could be components of this recommendation, depending on the preference and past experiences of the individual being supported). This section may also contain the recommendation for a Spiritual Life Companion if the individual does not have a family/community relationship actively engaged in their weekly life. We may also incorporate recommendations for specific mindfulness practices that may help to soothe some general anxiety for this person (e.g., mandalas, walks outside, enjoying the view from their back porch swing, etc.).